Just because people meet for a regularly scheduled church service does not mean that people have encountered the presence of God. In his new book, Pastor David Stewart takes us past the surface into the desperate need we all have to encounter God's presence. His transparency is refreshing and brings us face to face with this reality—outside of the presence of the living Christ, we will only have the trappings of Christianity.

Chresten Tomlin
Evangelist, Chresten Tomlin Ministries

Intimacy with God! Is it possible? Pastor David Stewart reminds us that not only is it possible, it is absolutely vital to the believer's relationship with God. That intimacy is foundational to the believer's effectiveness in fulfilling the purpose for which God placed us here. The garden of Eden was designed for intimacy. There, Adam and Eve walked with God in the cool of the evening. They were naked and not ashamed. Disobedience changed the relationship! How ironic that in the very place designed for intimacy, they hid from God. Ministry to the Lord precedes ministry for the Lord! No wonder that when Jesus called His disciples in Mark chapter 3, He "ordained" them—that they should (first) be with Him! Then, they were to go and preach the gospel, cast out demons, and heal the sick. Doing for comes out of being with! Is God weeping over us the way Christ wept over Jerusalem? "I have longed to gather you...but ye would not!" May David Stewart's words inspire all of us to seek the face of God—and not just His hand!

Robert Wise, Jr.
Southern New England Ministry Network Pastor

David Stewart, Jr. is one of the most sincere Christ followers I know. He has a heart for the truth of God's Word and a passion for teaching practical application of authentic spiritual experience. This message concerning the personal work of the Holy Spirit is much needed in the church today. It is a straight forward and clear encouragement to open our lives to the transforming and world-changing power of the Holy Spirit. When David writes about the Holy Spirit he is not writing about a concept or a principle, he is speaking out of an intimate relationship and life-long encounter. I was both encouraged and challenged, not because I learned things I had not heard before, but because the simplicity of the message in the context of the testimony of a life well lived encouraged me to seek the renewal of the Spirit in my life once again.

David Delp
Executive Secretary and Director of Leadership Development for the Indiana Assemblies of God

HUNGRY for

His PRESENCE

The Heart and Hope of Spiritual Renewal

DAVID E. STEWART, JR.

5 Fold Media
Visit us at www.5foldmedia.com

Hungry for His Presence: The Heart and Hope of Spiritual Renewal
Copyright © 2017 by David E. Stewart, Jr.
Published by 5 Fold Media, LLC
www.5foldmedia.com

All Scripture quotations, unless otherwise noted, are taken from the New American Standard Bible, Copyright 1960, 1962, 1963, 1968, 1971, 1972, 1973, 1975, 1977, 1995 by the Lockman Foundation, used by permission.

Scripture marked KJV are taken from the King James Version. Public Domain in the USA.

ISBN: 978-1-942056-56-0

Library of Congress Control Number: 2017956148

Printed in the USA

Dedication & Acknowledgments

One morning several years ago during a winter season in my life, the Lord awakened me with the instructions to write a book entitled *Hungry for His Presence.* After several years this book is now a reality. So it is with great thanksgiving that I dedicate this book to the almighty, living, and loving God.

The heavenly Father graciously and kindly saved me through faith in His dear Son Jesus Christ. He wonderfully filled me with His precious Holy Spirit, and He mercifully called me into His service. It is He who has created in me a deep desire to know Him. It is He who has given me the direction and leading to write this book. So it is to God that I dedicate this book, and it is to Him that I give all glory and honor and praise.

> *"For from Him and through Him and to Him are all things. To Him be the glory forever. Amen"* (Romans 11:36 NASB).

Further, I wish to give my friend and fellow minister, Evangelist Pat Schatzline, a word of appreciation. Pat is a man of commitment and dedication to the Lord Jesus. He has encouraged me in this process and put me in touch with my publishers. Thank you, Pat. Keep up the good work for Jesus.

Finally, I wish to thank Andy and Cathy Sanders and all the 5 Fold Media team. Thank you for inviting me to send the manuscript and for taking me into your tutelage. Thanks!

Contents

Come, let us return to the Lord. For He has torn us, but He will heal us; He has wounded us, but He will bandage us. He will revive us after two days; He will raise us up on the third day, that we may live before Him. So let us know, let us press on to know the Lord. His going forth is as certain as the dawn; and He will come to us like the rain, like the spring rain watering the earth (Hosea 6:1-3).

And blessed be His glorious name forever; and may the whole earth be filled with His glory (Psalms 72:19).

Now when Solomon had finished praying, fire came down from heaven and consumed the burnt offering and the sacrifices, and the glory of the LORD filled the house (2 Chronicles 7:1).

Foreword

Rarely have I read a book that so ministered to my spirit personally as this message from heaven that you now hold in your hands. This book is an Isaiah 58:1, "Cry aloud, and spare not" book written as a trumpet blast to the bride and the wandering saint by my dear friend pastor and missionary David E. Stewart, Jr. I believe that David is cut from a cloth that was fashioned by Jesus and that was hemmed by the Holy Spirit. The authority and passion that he writes with could only come from a man who walks with a limp called "brokenness" and a deep relationship with the Father. This book awakened dormant areas that God had long desired to fill within my own life. In fact, as I read the book *Hungry for His Presence,* I found myself alone in the cleft of the rock waiting for Jesus to walk by.

This book is a wake-up call! This is a day when much of the church is satisfied with microwave Christianity, altar-less services, and humanistic feel-good messages from the pulpit. I truly believe that somewhere along the way we have reduced the Holy Spirit to a doorman and not the orchestra director.

Hungry for His Presence

The depth at which we encounter God will always be determined by the passion with which we pursue Him. We must once again develop an appetite to go to the lonely place where Jesus can be found interceding on our behalf. Jesus promised us, "Ask and it will be given to you; seek and you will find; knock and the door will be opened to you" (Matthew 7:7). I truly believe that if the Devil cannot entice you to sin, then he will just make you busy! Enough already! We must become hungry again. Jesus declared in Matthew 5:6, "Blessed are those who hunger and thirst for righteousness, for they will be filled." This book will stir your heart and renew your spirit, but more importantly it will create a hunger for God that will only be satisfied in the secret place.

I encourage you to prepare yourself as you embark on reading this book. Savor every page as if it is your last meal before a long journey. This book is destined to be in the library of every person who understands that without Jesus we are mere mortals lost without a compass. Be prepared to shout from the rooftops Romans 1:16: "For I am not ashamed of the gospel, because it is the power of God that brings salvation to everyone who believes: first to the Jew, then to the Gentile."

Pat Schatzline, Evangelist and Author
Remnant Ministries International

Prologue

"Those who have once tasted the
Shekinah of God in daily experience
can never again live satisfied without
'the practice of the presence of God.'"
— Richard Foster[1]

Physical and emotional weariness had nearly overwhelmed me after many successive weeks of itinerate evangelistic ministry across the nation. It was a Sunday night, and I finally had an evening off. Hoping for renewal and refreshment, I decided to visit a large church in the city where my wife and I were residing.

The church was beautiful with its cross-topped steeple pointing majestically to the sky. After slipping into the entrance and passing through an oversized lobby designed to aid movement and flow of parishioners, I entered the spacious, warmly colored sanctuary. The auditorium lights were dimmed, but the singers on stage were bathed in brilliant red and white beams

---

1. Richard J. Foster, *Celebration of Discipline* (New York: HarperCollins Publishers, 1998), 162.

of spotlights and strobes. They sang enthusiastically, moving and dancing to the pulse of the beat. As the mood of the music changed, the bright lights faded into cool blues and muted yellows to capture the nuances of the slower songs that followed.

After a short prayer and an offering, the pastor rose to speak. He was eloquent—unusually eloquent—speaking slowly and deliberately with a slight southern drawl. After announcing and reading his biblical text, he described elite military troops' commitment to their team and to victory. He spoke with the measured cadence of a man practiced in the art of preaching. His sermon evoked images of a coach challenging his team before a championship game. The pastor ended his homily with an emotionally laden illustration and a quiet appeal to unity. Then, after a short prayer, the service was finished.

Slipping out of the sanctuary, I passed back through the lobby, now bustling and noisy with congregants, and found my way to my car in the gigantic parking lot. After a quiet ride back to the place where we were staying, I entered and silently sat at a small wooden table, where I wept uncontrollably.

"What's wrong?" my wife asked. There was no immediate reply. When I did finally speak, I could not communicate the depth of what I felt. Although I had gone to church hoping to find spiritual renewal and emotional refreshment, I had returned disappointed and weary. Now, I was unable to adequately explain the reason for my tears and dismay; indeed, the depth of my own feelings seemed inexpressible. There was no doubting the commitment of the worship team, nor did I suspect the sincerity of the pastor, but something was missing. And so, I cried as a man who has been deeply wounded.

A few months later, I spent a long, emotional but wonderful day visiting with a dear friend. His wife, a precious and loving woman, had passed away only weeks earlier, and our conversation reflected the sorrow of his great loss. He candidly opened his heart and shared his pain and story with lucidity and transparency. We laughed, cried, and shared stories and precious memories.

Sometime during that day, as our thoughts and conversation wandered through a gamut of feelings and expressions, our discussions turned to eternal things and spiritual concerns.

"Dave," I asked, "what is the greatest need of our church today?" My question reflected deep appreciation for his spirituality and revealed the respect that I have for him as a state-level leader in our denomination.

Dave paused for a moment in his thoughtful way and answered, "I cannot speak for our church nationally, but on a local level there are two things that I see. There is a need for discipleship and there is a deep need for the presence of God."

Hungry for His Presence

In that brief moment, I had the simple answer to my feelings of emptiness, disappointment, and hunger that I had recently experienced when I left the church service that Sunday night. What I needed— what I hungered for and longed for—was the presence of God. I didn't need another inspirational or motivational message. Professionally produced programs and emotionally laden songs cannot meet our deepest longings. The human heart craves the presence of the Almighty. Nothing else matters. Only His presence can satisfy the hunger, quench the thirst, and refresh the weary spirit.

This book is, therefore, about the presence of God— the presence of God in an individual's life and the presence of God in the life of the church, the body of Christ. It is written from the heart of a hungry man, a thirsty man, a man desperate for the presence of God.

Are you hungry for the presence of God? Are you longing for a deeper sense of His glory and power in your own life or in the life of your church? If you hunger and thirst for God's presence, long for revival and refreshment, I invite you to join me on this journey—this treasure hunt for the presence of the living God.

Chapter 1

Are You Satisfied?

"I am sorry to say this, but too much of what we call Christian is not a manifestation of the supernatural life of God in our souls. Too much of what we call Christian is really just human."
— Dallas Willard[2]

The church where I gave my heart to Jesus was small, with perhaps 150 regular attendees. The congregation was made up of simple people—farmers and blue-collar workers. Parishioners with names like Aunt Betty, "Sister" Turner, and Buck all attended faithfully alongside Granddaddy Perry and my sweet and godly grandmother.

Do you know what I remember most about that church? There was a very powerful sense of the presence of God throughout the worship services.

---

2. Dallas Willard, The Great Omission: Reclaiming Jesus's Essential Teachings on Discipleship (New York: HarperCollins Publishers, 2006), 51.

Hungry for His Presence

Sometimes the aura of the Holy Spirit was so strong that I was, on one hand, eager for more, while on the other I was a little afraid of something so awesome my young mind could not comprehend it.

It was there on a Sunday night, when I was a young child, that I gave my heart to Jesus. The presence of God made all the difference. Yet, not all my church experiences were so blessed.

There was another church that I often attended when I was a little boy. I was the eldest son of missionaries and a young student in a boarding school, where services were conducted in a small but beautiful stone church building. I was forced to attend the services where I was bored and disengaged. The ceremonies felt unbearably long and were characterized by lengthy recitals of prayers and sermons that neither captured my attention nor seemed relevant to my daily life. The religious formalities that were often associated with those church experiences never impressed me.

In fact, my greatest church-related joy in those days was to be chosen as one of two young boys who pumped the bellows for the grand pipe organ that was installed behind the altar table. When our duty was completed, we were able to slip out of the church and meander about for a few minutes before a teacher ushered us into the back of the sanctuary for the remainder of the service.

David Stewart

No, I am not longing for the formality of religious dogma and creeds; on the other hand, neither am I advocating for the informality that characterizes many contemporary services. My plea is not for a return to traditional hymns, nor is it an argument for contemporary expressions of worship. My spirit simply craves an opportunity to meet with God, fellowship with Him, and receive His healing peace.

There is a deep, insatiable hunger for God within me—a desire to be engulfed in His presence and surrounded by His glory. Style is not as important as substance. Aesthetic beauty, décor, and ambiance are neither as important nor deeply desired as the splendor of His presence. While I appreciate skill and talent, I am not at all thirsty for professionalism—I am thirsty for God.

I am hungry for His presence because of the difference it makes in my life. On one hand, His presence does not necessarily make me feel good about myself—sometimes, quite the contrary. When I have been disobedient to God's Word, His presence makes me tremble and cry out for mercy. His presence causes me to hate my selfishness, self-centeredness, and basest desires. His presence makes me uncomfortable as He confronts my rebellion and disobedience to His Word and commands.

On the other hand, when I have repented and have sincerely surrendered to Jesus, His presence brings joy and wholeness. He cures my brokenness caused

19

by emotional pain inflicted by others. His presence heals my diseases that abound in this sin-ravaged world, and mends my wounded heart which is empty without Him.

His presence is transformational. When I am truly in His presence, my old nature—characterized by selfishness, greed, pride, impatience, and intemperance[3]—is transformed into His nature and His character. He fills me with Himself and transforms me into His likeness, filling me with peace, joy, and love.

His presence causes me to bow in worship. In His presence, I recognize His grandeur, holiness, power, beauty, and love. His presence makes me catch a glimpse of His greatness, which causes me to desperately long for His touch and smile of approval.

---

3. 2 Corinthians 14:20

Chapter 2

Are You Running?

A man talks to himself when he is forsaken and lonely in a wilderness. Moses found himself alone, with the exception of a flock of sheep and the occasional wild creature, which haunted the desert places where he labored, tending the wealth of his father-in-law.

It is hard to find reasons to talk when you are alone shepherding bleating, grazing sheep; it is even harder to dream big dreams or have great ambitions when you are in the desert with little to no hope of going anywhere else. This is especially true when you have escaped to the desert from a place where there is a bounty on your head.

Moses never dreamed of being a shepherd when he was a young boy or teenager. He dreamed of leading his people into freedom and national glory. He dreamed of helping the helpless and delivering slaves from injustice and oppression.

Hungry for His Presence

Moses' earlier life in Egypt was one of apparent paradox. He was born into the home of slaves with the pall of a murderous death sentence cast over him and his family. There was little hope of his life being extended beyond a few days or hours. He was condemned to die, not for any crime but for the simple fact that he was of the wrong ancestry—the wrong race and the wrong gender. Other boys from his community were being exterminated like helpless rodents at the hands of their Egyptian masters, and there was no apparent reason that he would be spared beyond a few tortuous hours of psychological pain and emotional agony for his mother and family.

Yet, through an act of despair scented with the slightest air of faith, his mother and older sister hid him amongst the reeds of the Nile River. His life was not only spared, it was elevated to a place of regal advantage beyond the imagination of his poor, oppressed parents. By an act of God— an unexplainable miracle involving the unlikely compassion and mercy of an Egyptian princess—he became a prince of the land, enjoying royalty, riches, and comfort. Above all else, he gained access to the highest levels of education found in Egypt, the most powerful nation in the world at that time.

Except for one factor, Moses would have spent his childhood living in Pharaoh's palace oblivious to his heritage and the suffering that would have been his if he had survived and lived in the home of his parents who were Jewish slaves. God caused his adoptive parent, Pharaoh's daughter, to choose his own mother to be his nurse. His mother fed him, bathed him, gave him moral instruction, and told him of the injustice that the Egyptians forced on their Jewish slaves, while her hands, rough from brick-making, caressed him, and her soft, loving eyes filled with pain-induced tears.

Moses could have pushed his mother's tender admonitions and teaching out of his consciousness. He could have enjoyed the luxury afforded the Egyptian monarchy and chosen a place of prominence as a leader while ignoring the plight of his family and people. He could have, but he did not.

Anger began to build inside Moses. Resentment was quickly developing toward those who had on one hand helped him, but on the other abused his people, even his own parents and family. He hated the prejudice, meanness, and discrimination that he witnessed daily as the Egyptian slave masters tormented his people, his own flesh and blood.

At the same time, Moses started feeling a sense of destiny and life purpose. He felt that God had spared him and raised him up for a purpose. He believed that God had ordained him to be a leader and a deliverer for His people.[4] Moses did not fully understand what was happening to him, but the call of God was

---

4. Acts 7:25

beginning to reveal itself in Moses' heart and mind in intense and passionate ways.

What do we mean by the term "the call of God"? Charles Greenaway, a great missionary statesman, and mentor to me, once said, "Son, we are all called with the same calling." He did not elaborate on what he meant, but I have given much thought to it. My understanding of "the call" has been modified as I have meditated on the scriptural directive to become disciples of Jesus Christ.

As Jesus called His disciples inviting them to "Follow Me,"[5] so Jesus calls *us* to follow Him. He does so by the beckoning power and voice of His Holy Spirit. We make a decision to follow Jesus when we hear the news of His death and resurrection and sense the invitation of the Spirit to follow Him. In doing so, we surrender our wills, desires, and ambitions to the Lord Jesus, choosing to do His will and to live in obedience to His Word. So then, we are all called with the same calling—to follow Jesus in discipleship.

When we embark on that journey, we begin learning about Jesus and continually make choices to obey His commandments. In the midst of those discipleship processes, Jesus often gives us directives and commands to reach out to others in ministry. We often say that those instructions from the Lord to

5. Matthew 4:19

24

engage in specific ministries are "the call of God" or "the call to ministry."

The call to ministry often reveals our life purpose and helps us understand God's present and future plans for our lives. It also helps us discover our God-given gifts and talents that enable us to fulfill His purposes and plans for our lives. Thus, the call of God is critical and essential in the life of a man or woman of God. Yet, without the presence of God, the dreams and call have little meaning and certainly have no discernable impact.

One day, as anger and a sense of destiny collided, passion erupted in Moses' heart when he, the young, adopted Egyptian prince, went to visit the place where his kin lived and labored. More than likely, he had visited before and had witnessed the brutality of the slave masters as they drove the slaves to cruel labor. This particular day, he had once again seen an Egyptian abusing a Jewish slave. In a moment of unrestrained anger, Moses killed the Egyptian and quickly disposed of the body beneath the desert sand. He thought that no one was witness to his impulsive deed.

The following day, Moses returned to the scene of his crime and happened upon two slaves fighting. He attempted to intervene, scolding the men for their brawl, but was quickly rebuffed and rebuked as one man recalled the previous day's incident. Moses was surprised and filled with anxiety. He thought the

Jewish people would ascertain his calling to deliver them and accept his authority over them, but the slave challenged him saying, "Who made you a ruler and judge over us?"[6] Responding in fear and depression, Moses fled for his life.

Moses had the seed of God's call in his heart. He felt that he had a destiny and that his life had been spared for that future purpose. He was meant to be a leader; he was destined to be a deliverer of God's people. Moses had a passionate dream, but something went wrong that day; something—that is, Someone—was missing.

The circumstances of Moses' life at that moment seemed to indicate that his dream would never become reality. Pharaoh and his Egyptian loyalists had violently turned against Moses—even threatening his life. His own people whom he loved and wanted to help did not recognize his call and even questioned his authority to assist them. Neither the Egyptians nor the Israelites believed in Moses and his dream of leadership or the call that he felt God had given him. Eventually, Moses also questioned his dreams and fled his call—perhaps denying that he ever had one.

How many pastors, deacons, elders, and ministry leaders have had experiences just like Moses? They have had a passionate dream, believing that they are called into ministry and into Christian leadership

6. Acts 7:27

positions. A zealous sense that God designed purpose and meaning for their life filled their hearts. They have studied and prepared themselves for leadership. They have attended conferences to educate and equip themselves. Some have even had prophetic words spoken over their lives confirming their dreams and call. Yet circumstances have caused doubt and fear to fill their hearts. A moment of passion or zeal has cast a shadow over their lives and ministry. People who have turned against them have brought emotional pain and spiritual anxiety into their hearts and minds.

Further, many of these same men and women of God faithfully pray and minister to the needs and burdens of their people, yet they feel lonely and empty. Ministers fill pulpits and preach messages prepared with hours of study, but their preaching yields no results. Workers visit needy homes and distribute food, clothing, or toys to people who do not express appreciation nor change their self-destructive lifestyles. Something is indeed missing. They have passion and a call. They even possess superb talent and indisputable qualifications, but where is God? As a result, emptiness, loneliness, and purposelessness haunt their dreams and slowly chip away the assurance of their calling, and God seems a thousand miles away.

These faithful Christian workers attempt good deeds with sincere hearts, but their valiant efforts and their earnest spirits become wearied and empty as they labor without acknowledgement or appreciation and, most importantly, without the approval of God's powerful presence. They try to do helpful, substantial things, but their efforts are born of futility without God's blessings. Those they hope to help reject them, and their colleagues ignore or even refute them. Hopes and dreams are shattered one day and one failure at a time.

Like Moses, they are not sure what went wrong or why they have failed. So, they resign the pastorate, quit the ministry, and escape the scene of their failure. Their dreams have become nightmares. There is something missing, but they are not sure what they lack or what they need. So, like Moses, they run. They scurry from Pharaoh, from Egypt, and from God's people. Above all, they dash away from their dreams, no longer assured that God had any part in them.

Are you running—or at least wanting to run—from your call, denying that you ever had grand, God-given dreams? Do you feel your feet are on slippery soil with no spiritual traction or strength? Are you hungry for God but feel that He is a thousand miles away? If so, keep reading! God is near—even in the wilderness when you can't feel His presence. He is close at hand and wants to remind you that He has called you and that the dream, once so real in your heart, was a God-inspired dream designed to lead you to His purposes and plans for your life.

Chapter 3

Are You Hiding?

"If you continue in My word, then you
are truly disciples of Mine."[7]

My father took me on an unforgettable camping and fishing trip when I was fifteen. We were living in India and our adventure began with a long car ride along a bumpy, curvy road that wound its way through dense tropical forests that were home to gaur (a large, bison-like animal), deer, wild chickens, wild cats, and other exotic creatures. We then hiked across hills covered with long, sharp-edged grass to a beautiful trout stream that gurgled along through the grassy and forested hillsides of the Western Ghats.

Upon arrival we set up a canvas tent and rolled out our sleeping bags hoping for some good rest before our fishing expedition the next day. We built a fire and

7. John 8:31

cooked some simple food before crawling into our bags and falling asleep.

The following day, we wakened early to a frosty mountain morning. We took a bath in the chilly water of a nearby waterfall cascading over huge boulders and then ate a quick breakfast of cold hard-boiled eggs and bread. Finally, we made our way down to the trout stream and began casting our lures into the beautiful, sparkling pools where the trout swam. I only caught one fish that day, a rainbow trout that we later cleaned and ate, but I will always remember that trip with my dad.

Dad and I were campers. Campers prepare for their experience, buying food and supplies that they hope will last the duration of their fun adventure.

Moses was not a camper. When he fled Egypt he did so as a fugitive. He was running from the law.

Fugitives don't typically enjoy their experience. People escaping from justice don't camp—they hide. They usually have not had much time to plan for their experience, and therefore they are not prepared to face the harsh conditions that await them.

Fugitives flee and fight to survive. They slip and slide into hidden places, eat what they can scavenge, and sleep under moss or rocks hoping to evade the searching eyes of those who wish to catch them.

David Stewart

When Moses fled Egypt in fear, he absconded knowing that Pharaoh Ramesses II,[8] the Egyptian despot, had placed a bounty on his head. Moses was afraid and fled for his life.

Perhaps he had a specific destination in mind when he scurried out of Egypt as a condemned and wanted criminal, but Holy Scripture does not imply that he knew where he was going. Rather, Scripture implies that he ran, living in the desert, surviving on skills he may have learned in military training provided by the Egyptians.

Moses hurried along ancient routes used by merchants, armies, and travelers, hiding at the sight of Egyptian soldiers who traveled the same roads. Presuming that he left from the ancient Egyptian city referred to in the Bible as Raamses,[9] Moses may have traveled by Bir Mara, across the northern edge of the Desert of Sinai, and southeast to Midian on the road that is known in modern times as the Darb el-Hagg.

After many difficult miles, Moses arrived in the land of Midian, an area east of the Gulf of Elath on the western edge of the Arabian Desert. Eventually, he happened upon a well that was used by the people of the area. Water was understandably difficult to find in that desert region and a valuable commodity for which men were willing to fight; therefore, it is not

8. Bill T. Arnold and Bryan E. Beyer, *Encountering the Old Testament* (Grand Rapids: Baker Academic, 1998), 108.

9. Exodus 1:11

surprising to read that shepherds who grazed and watered their flocks in that region tried to keep the daughters of Reuel, the priest of Midian, from drawing water from the well.[10]

Moses was witness to the shepherds' bullying ways and he intervened on behalf of the daughters of Reuel. Undoubtedly, the girls were appreciative of Moses' intervention and were perhaps enamored by the strong and courageous young man. When they returned home, the girls told their father about Moses and his act of valor. The man and his family invited Moses to Reuel's home where he was evaluated. Eventually, Moses was offered one of Reuel's daughters, Zipporah, in marriage. After the wedding, Moses served as a hireling shepherd for his father-in-law.

Moses had not dreamed of this life. He had often thought that he had been born with purpose. Yet, now he found himself a fugitive running from the law as a result of his passion and his burden—or more likely as a result of his impetuous action. Although Moses was married, he felt alone. Although he was employed, he was haunted by a suspicion that he had aborted his destiny. He had once dreamed with a sense of purpose but now felt incapable of ever realizing his goals in life. He was running and thought he could never go back because of his failures.

10. Exodus 2:16-18

Moses had run and was hiding. He had run from his call, his dreams, but above all, he had run from God. The next step of Moses' journey would help him turn the corner and eventually lead him back to his dream and his calling, but most importantly it would take him back to the source of his call. Moses would have an encounter with God that would remove him from the hiding place and put him back into a place with God where his dreams would become reality.

Are you hiding from your failures, your fears, or your haters and doubters? Do you feel alone? Does failure trouble your memories and condemn your future? Have your dreams turned into nightmares?

Are you hiding? If so, perhaps you need a fresh encounter with God—another glimpse of His power and might. You may need to spend time in His presence where your dreams can be revived, your call renewed, and your hopes restored.

Chapter 4

Have You Encountered God?

"The perpetual presence of the Lord (omnipresence, as we say) moves from a theological dogma into a radiant reality."
— Richard Foster[11]

One day Moses, alone and discouraged, was watching his sheep as they wandered about looking for tufts of grass springing up between the rocks of the vast desert landscape. He had neither a sense of expectation nor a hope of change in his life. He felt condemned to be a lowly shepherd, subjected and subservient to his father-in-law.

Perhaps he was sitting mindlessly in the shade of a large rock when he slowly lifted his eyes to look in the direction of an unusual sound that interrupted his reverie. He might have thought it was the sound of a

11. Foster, *Celebration*, 19.

sheep stumbling or falling. Raising his eyes, however, he saw a bush that was burning in the distance.

He rose with a sense of mild curiosity to investigate. He had probably seen fires like that before, as the hot desert sun combined with the low humidity of that arid region sometimes caused such bushes to burst spontaneously into flame. As he moved toward the bush, he may have felt thankful that something had broken his boredom, but he was certainly not expecting to have an encounter with God. His complacency was immediately shattered when God spoke, saying:

> *"Do not come near here; remove your sandals from your feet, for the place on which you are standing is holy ground." He said also, "I am the God of your father, the God of Abraham, the God of Isaac, and the God of Jacob." Then Moses hid his face, for he was afraid to look at God.*[12]

An overwhelming fear enveloped Moses. He had never encountered the presence of God before and stood trembling as God spoke to him. It is a fearful thing to stand unclean and sinful before the almighty, Holy God.

Moses met God, and he would forever be changed.

12. Exodus 3:5-6

We don't know much about Moses' personal faith during his childhood and young formative years. In fact, we really do not know much about his faith during his young adult years. It is usually assumed that his mother taught him about the God of Abraham, Isaac, and Jacob; however, if Moses had been religious or held religious convictions as a child or young adult, he may have set them aside during the fearful and lonely years of exile in Midian. If he had ever thought about God or had faith in Him at all, the desert and the dirty, bleating sheep had probably made him forget most of what his mother ever taught him.

God broke into Moses' lonely reverie with words full of significance and instruction: *"Do not come near here; remove your sandals from your feet, for the place on which you are standing is holy ground."*[13] Moses quickly learned that God was extra-ordinary, supremely sacred, and entirely holy. He could not be ignored or treated casually. God was not to be regarded as one would treat a common friend, nor was He to be approached as one would enter the presence of a dignitary or of royalty.

God told Moses to remove his shoes in order to teach him the ethical and moral superiority of God over man. If Moses was ever going to learn to enjoy the presence of God, he would first need to honor His presence and give Him the respect He deserved. Moses could not casually entertain the presence of God. God is holy and must be

---

13. Exodus 3:5

recognized and honored for His total holiness. He cannot and will not be treated as common. He has no equal.

As Moses learned to revere and honor God, so anyone who wishes to be used by God must first discover how to respect God privately and publicly. This is particularly important in light of western egalitarianism.

Egalitarianism is a philosophy of life that regards all people as equal in value and deserving of equal consideration in all areas of life. It particularly emphasizes economic, political, and social equality. This philosophy has some roots in ancient Greek culture but has found fertile soil in the minds and hearts of western philosophers and has captured the cultural imagination of the vast majority of western society.

Egalitarianism has fostered an attitude of commonness in the minds of many westerners. This philosophy of life has influenced every area of life and thought. It has impacted communication, lifestyle, and relationships. Egalitarianism is evidenced in language patterns, fashion and style, and the way that people relate to one another in both social and work settings. Western culture has evolved into one of uniformity.

While these cultural trends do not intrinsically promote sinful behaviors or ungodly attitudes, they have altered perspectives on religion and spiritual practices. Furthermore, religious language has been challenged, and in an attempt to culturally

David Stewart

contextualize Scripture many words have been changed or deleted.

Sometimes, it seems that God does not deserve any more respect than we give each other or authority figures such as police officers and school teachers. Modern terminology and theology tend to promote the personification rather than the deification of God.

As egalitarian and humanistic ideas have flourished, some church leaders have become afraid of offending people or of making people feel uncomfortable. As a result, they do not talk about sin or the judgment of God. They are reluctant to talk about the cross of Christ or of Jesus' shed blood.

Church leaders who may be reluctant to confront people about their sins and their real spiritual need choose instead to preach about people's felt needs. They want people to feel valuable, needed, non-threatened, and relaxed.

The only problem with this is that people's greatest need is usually not one of their felt needs. Their greatest need is the need that they are usually least aware of—their need for a Savior.

People need a Savior because they are sinners, but many have no understanding of sin or its consequences. The mistake that we often make is that we speak of sin in the context of human behavior or culturally accepted norms rather than in light of God's commands. So, eventually people judge themselves and their conduct by the actions and lifestyles of their neighbors, friends, and acquaintances.

On the other hand, when we encounter the presence of God we stop comparing ourselves with others and begin seeing ourselves in the light of the Almighty, the Holy One. We begin to realize that God speaks about sin in His Word from the perspective of His divine nature and in the framework of His holy commands. In the holy place of His presence and in the pages of His Word, one becomes acutely aware of personal sin.

Moses quotes God saying, "You shall be holy, for I am holy."[14] In the New Testament, Peter reiterates this message by writing, "Like the Holy One who called you, be holy yourselves also in all your behavior; because it is written, 'You shall be holy, for I am holy.'"[15]

Furthermore, many churches are afraid of any radical manifestation of the presence of God. They are afraid people will "freak out" if God shows up in the physical or emotional response of congregants to God's presence. Yet, we see that just as Moses' encounter with God caused him to face his own spiritual inadequacy, when people encounter God today they begin to catch a glimpse of His glory and majesty. They realize that He is greater than our preconceived ideas, holier than our twisted humanized concepts of deity, and mightier than our imaginations can possibly fathom.

14. Leviticus 11:45
15. 1 Peter 1:15-16

David Stewart

The psalmist proclaims, "The Lord reigns, He is clothed with majesty."[16] The same psalm continues, "Holiness befits Your house, O Lord, forevermore."[17] God deserves—indeed He demands—our respect, obedience, and worship, but we can never understand that if we do not have a life-changing encounter with Him.

God called the Old Testament prophet Isaiah to prophesy to the nation of Judah, challenging the people to repent of their sins and return to true faith and obedience to God. Isaiah recalls a vision of God's grandeur and His glory that prepared him for the prophetic ministry that he was to have to the nation. He writes, "I saw the Lord sitting on a throne, lofty and exalted, with the train of his robe filling the temple."[18] That vision of God caused Isaiah to proclaim, "Woe is me, for I am ruined! Because I am a man of unclean lips, and I live among a people of unclean lips."[19]

Before Isaiah could confront the sins of the nation, he first had to acknowledge his own sins. He would have self-righteously and arrogantly condemned others for their evil unless he had first been humbled in the presence of the almighty, holy God, whose holiness sets the standard for all people to follow and imitate. Judah's sinfulness was not to be compared to the

16. Psalms 93:1
17. Psalms 93:5
18. Isaiah 6:1
19. Isaiah 6:5

41

self-righteousness of a religious man but was to be revealed in contrast to the holiness of God.

The apostle Paul, formerly Saul the Pharisee, was once filled with self-importance, self-assurance, and self-righteousness. He was extremely religious and had an attitude of superiority that caused him to hate and kill early followers of Jesus Christ.

Then, Paul had an encounter with Jesus and was never the same. He was no longer an arrogant, religious man who disdained others. He became contrite, humble, and even subservient to others. He would later write, "It is a trustworthy statement, deserving full acceptance, that Christ Jesus came into the world to save sinners, among whom I am foremost of all."[20] That revelation of his own sinfulness was not a result of his religious training or self-awareness. It came as a result of Paul's encounter with the living Lord Jesus. Jesus' presence convicted Paul when nothing else could. The presence of God convicts sinners and brings them to true repentance.

Churches without the presence of God want to make people comfortable and accepted, but the authors of Holy Scripture do not coddle people who are willfully living in disobedience. In fact, they do not speak kindly or lovingly to them or of them. Psalms 5:4-6 reads:

> *For You are not a God who takes pleasure in wickedness; no evil dwells with You.*

20. 1 Timothy 1:15

The boastful shall not stand before Your eyes; You hate all who do iniquity. You destroy those who speak falsehood; the Lord abhors the man of bloodshed and deceit.

Psalms 11:5-6 warns sinners saying:

The Lord tests the righteous and the wicked, and the one who loves violence His soul hates. Upon the wicked He will rain snares; fire and brimstone and burning wind will be the portion of their cup.

Paul the apostle warns the Romans by stating, "For the wages of sin is death."[21] Paul sacrificed his life for the sake of the gospel and unashamedly announced his love for both the saved and the unsaved, but he did not lower the bar of expectations, nor did he excuse the sins of the immoral and ungodly. Rather, Paul commanded that people in the church who were sexually immoral either repent or be removed from the church.[22]

David writes, "Tremble, and do not sin."[23] Psalms 99:1 reads, "The Lord reigns, let the peoples tremble."

21. Romans 6:23
22. 1 Corinthians 1-2
23. Psalms 4:4

43

Hungry for His Presence

Psalms 29:2 exhorts us to "Ascribe to the Lord the glory due His name."

Sinners cannot feel comfortable in the presence of God, nor should they be able to sit comfortably in our services without any awareness of their desperate spiritual need. Like Isaiah, they must tremble before God in fear. Like Moses, they must remove the filth and dirt from their lives. Only then can they rejoice in salvation and begin to walk in the power of His abiding Spirit.

An experience such as this will not come as the result of preaching that condemns or demands a legalistic way of life. Moses did not tremble in the sight of God because someone told him that he should do so. Isaiah did not come to a deep spiritual revelation of God's holiness and his own utter sinfulness because an itinerant preacher pointed out his miserable failures. John did not fall to the ground on the Isle of Patmos because he was shamed into a confession by a religious zealot. Conversely, such dramatic conversions come when a person encounters the presence of God.

It was a Sunday night and I was just a child, about eleven years old, when I first remember feeling the presence of God. I had gone to church with my family and was seated somewhere near the back of the small, wooden-framed country church. The pastor of that rural congregation had served as an evangelist before taking the pastorate, and his preaching still bore the characteristic style and message of his earlier ministry. He preached with zeal and fervor. As his preaching came to an end, I began to feel something I had never felt before. I was just a child, and in many respects I was still naïve and innocent; yet, that day, when I first felt the presence of God, I had an overwhelming sense that I was a sinner and in desperate need of salvation.

As the pastor finished his sermon, he called the worshipers forward to find a place of prayer around the front of the sanctuary, and many believers moved forward gathering around old-fashioned wooden altar railings. My mother joined the others as they moved forward to find a place to pray, but she slipped into the second or third row of the church before kneeling to pray.

The congregants began praying; however, I remained seated in the hard wooden pew. Yet, I was deeply disturbed. There was, on one hand, a sense of dread, and on the other spiritual hunger. I was aware of something that night that I had never sensed before.

Slowly, but determinedly, I got out of my seat, making my way down the center aisle until I came to the row where my mother was praying. I moved sideways toward her, slowly knelt by her side, tapped her on her shoulder, and asked, "Mom, will you pray for me?"

"Why?"

"I am a sinner, and I want to be saved."

Hungry for His Presence

The presence of God made me conscious of my sin. I knew that I needed forgiveness. Mother led me in a simple prayer of repentance and faith. After prayer, I walked away with a knowledge and joy that I was a child of the Father and that I had begun a living relationship with God. That moment was a pivotal moment in my life that not only brought me into a relationship with God but also initiated a thirst for His presence that increased as I matured in relationship.

Today, I am deeply convinced that the presence of God still convicts people of their sin. People who are godless and sinful are convicted of their ungodly deeds and lifestyles when they first encounter God's presence. People who have never felt pricked in their conscience for the way they live suddenly feel an overwhelming sense of their own wickedness when God comes near.

The challenge for the church today is not for greater professionalism, more skill, or better performances. Though such attributes can contribute to a meaningful worship experience and can help attract seekers, they can never be substitutes for the presence of God. The great need today is for people to encounter God in the house of God.

Chapter 5

What Are You Afraid Of?

The Lord said, "I have surely seen the affliction of My people who are in Egypt, and have given heed to their cry because of their taskmasters, for I am aware of their sufferings. So I have come down to deliver them from the power of the Egyptians, and to bring them up from that land to a good and spacious land, to a land flowing with milk and honey."[24]

In Moses' youth, he watched broken-hearted as his people bore the abuse of their Egyptian slave masters. He shook with anger at their exploitation. He was moved and determined to do something to help them—to free them.

Moses had once dreamed about being a deliverer for his people. He had at one time thought that he would be their leader. He used to dream of leading God's people back to their land of heritage and promise, but

24. Exodus 3:7-8

47

now he was just a lonely shepherd herding sheep in desert places.

As the dry desert sand swallows rainwater, the wilderness saps a man's strength and extracts the vision from his heart. Loneliness and a deep sense of failure haunted him, and it seemed that his dreams and ambition had been buried in the barren wasteland.

Now, the message that God gave Moses began to stir the dreams that had lain like embers in Moses' dry soul. The burden that he had once carried for his people suddenly came to life as God spoke.

When God is present and when He speaks, everything comes to life. Even dead things live when God speaks. The dream that had lain dormant in Moses' spirit and soul for so long began to revive.

God's words began to awaken old feelings and desires. Then, God spoke again. What He said next was a fearful thing. It confronted the deadness of Moses' soul. God's words challenged the lies of time and circumstances that had caused Moses to doubt his purpose and stop dreaming.

> *Therefore, come now, and I will send you to Pharaoh, so that you may bring My people, the sons of Israel, out of Egypt.*[25]

25. Exodus 3:10

Immediately, doubts and fears arose. Old pictures and images of past failures flashed through his mind. Once confident, his mind and heart were now fearful and dubious. Moses expressed his fear by asking, *"Who am I, that I should go to Pharaoh, and that I should bring the sons of Israel out of Egypt?"*[26]

Remember, Moses was a fugitive. He had left Egypt under threat of death. He had once been somebody, but now he was nobody. What could a simple shepherd do? How could he go back to Egypt? God responded to Moses with a promise: *"Certainly I will be with you."*[27]

God would go with Moses. God would accompany him back to his place of failure and would surround and protect him. God's presence would be with him, and that would make all the difference. Moses could start again—not alone this time, but with the presence of God.

What are you afraid of? What fears have killed your dreams and defeated your purpose? He says to you that He will go with you. You can start anew surrounded by His presence. You have nothing to be afraid of—God is with you.

What then shall we say to these things? If God is for us, who is against us?[28]

---

26. Exodus 3:11
27. Exodus 3:12
28. Romans 8:31

Chapter 6

What Is Your Weakness? What Limits You?

God promised Moses that He would be with him. Although that should have been enough assurance, Moses' fear persisted. He expressed his loss of confidence by saying:

> *Please, Lord, I have never been eloquent, neither recently nor in time past, nor since You have spoken to Your servant; for I am slow of speech and slow of tongue.* [29]

Moses expressed a deep-seated doubt and lack of self-assurance.

Stephen, one of the first deacons, referred to Moses in a speech he made just before he died by saying, "*Moses was educated in all the learning of the Egyptians, and he was a man of power in words and deeds.*"[30]

29. Exodus 4:10
30. Acts 7:22

Hungry for His Presence

Moses? Eloquent? When was that? We have been taught that Moses stammered.

How do we account for the seeming contradiction between what Stephen said about Moses and what Moses said about himself? Perhaps the question can be satisfied by a close examination of the circumstances in which Moses found himself when God spoke to him from the burning bush.

First, perhaps the power and eloquence that Stephen spoke of was evidenced when Moses killed the Egyptian taskmaster. As a result of that deed, however, Pharaoh had threatened Moses' life and caused Moses to flee from Egypt. Now a fugitive, Moses was never sure whether Pharaoh might send soldiers to search for him. Fear, his constant companion, may have dogged his every movement and filled his waking moments with anxiety. Fear takes a lot out of a man. It is difficult for a scared man to talk.

Second, as he took up the duties of a shepherd for his father-in-law, he spent long days and hours searching for grazing land for the sheep. As a result, he was forced to endure separation from his wife and the companionship that she offered. He was lonely with no one to talk to and no one to fellowship with. He was forced to find solace and comfort alone as he moved the sheep from one sparse grazing area to another. Loneliness devastates a man. It plays tricks with his mind so that he finds himself uttering soliloquies but unable to talk when face to face with another human. A lonely man forgets how to talk.

Third, Moses had moved from the adulation reserved for a prince in a palace to the disdain given to a desert-dwelling shepherd. As an adopted son of royalty, he had once walked confidently with his head held high. A proud man is a confident man. Now, he had no prestige nor honor, and certainly no use for speeches nor eloquence. He was just a forgotten, lonely, and perhaps incompetent shepherd. He had failed! He was humiliated, and his confidence was shattered. A humiliated man stammers; he can't speak clearly.

So then, Moses' fear, loneliness, and sense of failure may have robbed him of confidence and the self-assurance he once possessed. He was no longer the formidable opponent in battle, nor was he the eloquent speaker that Egyptian education had trained him to be. Moses was alone in the desert with his father-in-law's sheep and was fearful and lonely, unable to face his fears or pursue his passion and purpose.

In the same way, some Christian leaders, pastors, deacons, Sunday school teachers, choir members, and worship leaders are shadows of their former selves. They are well-educated. Families and parishioners once encouraged and strengthened them, yet now, as a result of a moral failure, misunderstanding, malicious gossip, or numerous other reasons, they have found themselves incapable of facing their problems or unable to pursue their dreams. They feel a deep sense of failure, rejection, incompetence, fear, or loneliness. They can't talk, and they can't perform. Talents, once apparent, are lost and forgotten.

Such people are in an emotional desert, a wasteland—a barren place spiritually, emotionally, and often relationally. They are empty. They have lost their vision and feel they have no purpose beyond their mundane daily tasks. In the process, they forget their call, lose a sense of purpose, and psychologically wither. Like Moses, they settle for *following* sheep through the wilderness when they have been called *to lead* God's people to the Promised Land.

Listening to the bleating of sheep when you were designed to hear God's heartbeat is an empty life. Moses felt defeated and forgotten, but God had not forgotten Moses.

Despite Moses' personal failures, God still had a design and purpose for his life. His plans for Moses had not been drawn in error, nor would they be retracted. God was preparing Moses for the day when He would reveal Himself and His plan to him. Moses' greatest days were just ahead of him. His gifts would once again be visible for all to see.

Have you lost your strength and confidence? Have you decided that the dreams and desires you attributed to God's call and gifts in your life were just mirages in desert sand? Are you hungry for God, yet He seems nowhere to be found? Have youthful passions and ambitions given way to the present realities and drudgeries of everyday life? Do you feel like a lonely shepherd stuck behind bleating sheep?

If so, don't be afraid or discouraged. God is waiting to reveal Himself to you in a most unusual way. He will restore your gifts; His presence will make the difference in your life.

Just when you think all is lost, God will show up. Your desert will become a sanctuary—a common, disdained thorn bush will serve as an instrument for God's presence to attract and pull you back to Himself and into His purpose for your life. God has not forgotten you, nor has He misplaced the plans He designed for you.

The talents and abilities you have cast aside will be picked up and noticed once again. You have destiny in your life; you have a purpose.

God will meet you in your desert. Perhaps from the most common thing or in the most mundane moment, He will speak to you and call you to your purpose.

You may have to take your shoes off—humble yourself. You may have to circumcise your son—repent for sins committed or commands unheeded. You may have to take a long, frightening trip through the desert back to Egypt—take a risk and make a huge commitment—but your divine destiny will be fulfilled.

Hungry for His Presence

Read the word of the Lord to Moses, which is also for you:

> *The Lord said to him, "Who has made man's mouth? Or who makes him mute or deaf, or seeing or blind? Is it not I, the Lord? Now then go, and I, even I, will be with your mouth, and teach you what you are to say."*[31]

The talents and strength you lost will come back. You will see God's power and purposes fulfilled in your life. Now, receive the word of God spoken to Jeremiah—take it in faith.

> *"Before I formed you in the womb I knew you,*
> *And before you were born I consecrated you;*
> *I have appointed you a prophet to the nations."*
> *Then I said, "Alas, Lord God!*
> *Behold, I do not know how to speak,*
> *Because I am a youth."*
> *But the Lord said to me,*
> *"Do not say, 'I am a youth,'*
> *Because everywhere I send you, you shall go,*
> *And all that I command you, you shall speak.*
> *Do not be afraid of them,*
> *For I am with you to deliver you,"*
> *declares the Lord.*[32]

---

31. Exodus 4:11-12
32. Jeremiah 1:5-8

Chapter 7

Have You Received His Power?

My maternal grandmother, Rena Perry, was a God-fearing girl who attended a small evangelical church in eastern North Carolina. She sang in the church choir, was active in other church activities, and confessed to having a personal salvation experience through faith in Jesus through the ministry of that church.

Then, in the mid to late 1920s, when she was eighteen years old, a Pentecostal evangelist named Elizabeth Snow (who later married one Mr. White and became known as Sister Snow White) began holding revival meetings in a small storefront building about ten miles from my grandmother's home.

Rena's older sister, Mary Jane, began attending the meetings and soon invited my grandmother to join her. They would travel to the meetings by a horse-drawn wagon or in a Model T Ford, stopping along the way to pick up friends who also were drawn to the meetings. As they bumped down the simple rural roadway, the small group sang and worshiped the Lord in preparation for what they expected to happen in the service.

The services each night were led enthusiastically by Sister Snow White who preached, calling the people in attendance to a deeper and closer walk with Jesus through the infilling of the Holy Spirit. Snow White recounted an experience subsequent to salvation that she and other Pentecostals shared called the baptism of the Holy Spirit.

Snow White taught that the baptism of the Holy Spirit was an added, deeper dimension of the Christian life that empowered believers for service and ministry. She encouraged the attentive young people gathered to wait on the Lord in prayer until He filled them with the Holy Spirit as He had done in the early days of the church. She often referred to the book of Acts when declaring that believers could experience the same dynamic presence of God and miraculous power of the Holy Spirit as described in the second, tenth, and nineteenth chapters of Acts.

One night, while my grandmother and other young women were praying together in the storefront building, she was baptized in the Holy Spirit and spoke in tongues as the Spirit enabled her. As she continued praying and rejoicing in the Lord, she began singing a song about the hope of an eternal home in heaven that she had never heard before. That song became a theme for her life and a symbol of the hope that she had in Jesus.

Shortly thereafter, some of the elders from her former church came to her house for an ecclesiastical visit. My grandmother saw them coming and met them on the front porch of her small wooden-framed house. The men told her that she must recant her Pentecostal experience and forbade her from attending the Pentecostal services. They also threatened to remove her name from their church's membership if she did not heed their demands.

The Spirit of God helped my grandmother respond to the elders with love and grace. Because she had been saved in their church, she honored them and wanted to maintain Christian fellowship with them. Nevertheless, she was hungry for more of God than she had experienced in their church. She had experienced a taste of His presence that made her long for more.

Her response shamed them and they turned and walked away. To our knowledge, my grandmother's name was never removed from the church rolls. Her testimony was not diminished; rather, it increased so that it was known in her community that she was a godly, praying woman whose prayers were answered.

A few years later, Rena's husband—my grandfather, Lloyd—entered into the Pentecostal experience as well. He became a devoted follower of Christ and immediately evidenced a change of lifestyle. He stopped smoking cigars, going to the movie theater, and began attending church with his family as often as the church doors opened. The presence of God transformed and empowered my grandparents' home.

When Moses encountered God at the burning bush, not only was he forced to recognize the holy nature of God, but he also received empowerment for the task that God had defined for him. Moses was told to return to Egypt and Pharaoh to demand the release of the Israelite slaves.

That would have been a daunting task for any man, but Moses' history made the mission all the more difficult. Moses did not dare approach Pharaoh on human terms with man's resources. Moses would have surely been executed upon entering Egypt, let alone at the notion of going before the supreme leader of the land who was revered as a god. Moses needed the assurance of God's favor, power, and presence.

That day, during the encounter at the burning bush, God gave Moses two valuable gifts as evidence of His call and favor on Moses' life. First, God offered him His name as the authority with which Moses would enter Pharaoh's presence; second, God offered Moses visual evidence of the divine favor on his life. God empowered Moses to perform signs and wonders with the shepherd's rod that he held in his hand.

The presence of God satisfies the spiritual hunger of a person, and the presence of God enables that one to do what he or she otherwise is incapable of doing.

The early church expected signs and wonders to follow the preaching of the gospel. The apostles, evangelists, pastors, and even deacons believed that miracles were evidentiary proof to unbelievers that God was with them and that His favor was upon them. The Scripture records, *"And they went out and preached everywhere, while the Lord worked with them, and confirmed the word by the signs that followed."*[33]

The book of Acts tells many stories of miraculous healings, powerful instances of deliverance, and wonderful miracles of God's saving grace. Signs and wonders were evidenced in the ministries of Peter and Paul, who are considered fathers of the church; moreover, miracles were also seen through the prayers and preaching of Stephen, one of the first deacons. Acts records this witness: *"And Stephen, full of grace and power, was performing great wonders and signs among the people."*[34]

Early Pentecostal believers in the twentieth century believed that the same power encountered by the followers of Jesus in the book of Acts could be experienced in their time. They believed that miracles were to be expected when the gospel was

33. Mark 16:20
34. Acts 6:8

preached, but they also held to a deep conviction that the power of God came as a result of the infilling of the Holy Spirit. Their faith held that there is a direct correlation between the presence of God present in a follower of Christ's life and the operation of the supernatural gifts of the Spirit.

Different ministries and writers have compiled myriad stories recording miracles and healings as a direct result of God's power and presence in people's lives; however, some of the most powerful stories have been left unwritten. Unknown Christians, simple followers of Christ who have seen the power of God explosively manifested, testify of His power and presence in their own lives.

My paternal grandfather, Eugene Stewart, came to Christ as a young married man and received a powerful infilling of the Holy Spirit shortly after his salvation experience. He often shared personal testimonies of God's healing power in his own life with his grandchildren and family.

Paw-Paw, as we called him, worked in the naval shipyard of Norfolk, Virginia. He was saved and filled with the Spirit as a young, married adult with small children. He unashamedly shared the gospel with fellow workers and even conducted Bible studies with his peers during their lunch hour.

The lunchtime Bible study that began with just a handful grew to include a rather large crowd of Paw-

David Stewart

Paw's fellow workers. The Holy Spirit seemed to be drawing people to the meetings, but there was one man who refused to attend despite my grandfather's most earnest invitations and attempts to pull him in.

One day, Paw-Paw was working alongside the man on the gun turret of a ship. During the course of their work, the huge gun turret slipped off its place and fell onto the man's hand, immediately severing his thumb. My grandfather quickly placed the detached thumb back on the spot where it had been torn off, wrapped a shirt around the bloody hand, said a word of prayer, and rushed the man to the medical clinic. When they arrived, the shirt was soaked in blood, but when they removed the shirt the man's thumb was restored to the hand as if it had never been severed. This miracle convinced the man of Jesus' power and he surrendered his life to Christ.

The presence of God that accompanies the anointing of the Holy Spirit enables believers and empowers them to do the works of Christ. His presence draws unbelievers to Christ. Supernatural gifts accompany followers of Christ, helping them fulfill the callings and purposes that God has designed for their lives.

Moses had the seed of leadership from an early age. He had the passion that is so often associated with the call of God and the purposes that God places in a person's heart. Yet, the desire and vision to lead God's people was frustrated and empty until he

63

had a personal encounter with the living God who empowered him with supernatural gifts.

When He gives His servants a task, God equips, enables, and empowers them. God gave Moses a staff. That staff would forever remind Moses of his personal encounter with God when he had been equipped to do his life's work. God also wants to equip and empower you to do his life's work.

God wants to equip and empower you, preparing you for your assigned task. He is waiting to fill you with His wonderful presence and empower you with His gifts. You can expect the loving Father to fill you with His precious Holy Spirit when you ask Him..

Chapter 8

What Are You Hungry For?

D o you long for the presence of God and for the gifts of the Holy Spirit to be manifested in your life? Are you thirsty for the living water of God to flow in and out of you? Do you want God's presence in your life to be as evident to others as Moses' staff was to Pharaoh and the children of Israel? If so, your hunger can be satisfied, your longings granted, and your thirst quenched. Jesus says to the hungry, *"I am the bread of life; he who comes to Me will not hunger, and he who believes in Me will never thirst."*[35]

For your spiritual desire to be fulfilled, your hunger must be centered on Jesus—not on spiritual gifts or miracles, but on Jesus.

The Holy Spirit comes to glorify Jesus. You must cry out to Jesus in your zeal for the gifts of the Spirit and the tangible presence of God in your life, ministry, and church—making Him the focus of your worship and

35. John 6:35

desire. He is the answer to your hunger; His presence alone will satisfy you.

There are two keys to receiving the infilling and overflowing presence of the Holy Spirit. The Lord Jesus said, *"Blessed are those who **hunger** and **thirst** for righteousness, for they shall be satisfied."*[36]

God rewards hunger. He feeds the physically hungry and satisfies the spiritual hunger of His children.

Are you hungry for the presence of God in your life or church? God says you are blessed when you are hungry for Him, the life-giving Bread of Life. Your hunger is evidence that God's grace is upon you, and that strong spiritual desire you are beginning to feel is reason for you to begin to celebrate.

The Holy Spirit creates a desire in the hearts of God's children for a deeper and closer walk with Him. When the Holy Spirit begins to develop that inner desire in a person's life, that person will not be satisfied with a display of fleshly talent, creative presentations, or intellectual arguments.

God intervenes when His people cry out to Him with spiritual hunger and thirst for His presence. God moves on behalf of His people when they ask Him to do so. Jesus said, *"Until now you have asked for nothing in My name; ask and you will receive, so that your joy may be made full."*[37]

36. Matthew 5:6

37. John 16:24

David Stewart

The night I was filled with the Holy Spirit was a glorious night. Just a few days earlier, I had cut my foot while cutting grass. I was a sixteen-year-old who was awkward and self-conscious yet hungry for God. I was thirsty for the presence of God in my life.

Somehow, by the grace of God, a deep spiritual desire had filled my heart and soul when I was just a small child. As I mentioned earlier in this book, I was a missionary kid and attended a boarding school where our school officials and house-parents forced us to go to church. I was bored with the drudgery of the whole affair. On the other hand, when I was just a small second or third grader, I would sneak into a wooded area and pray, with tears, asking God to speak to me. I wanted to know God. He was placing an insatiable desire in my heart to know Him more.

That ever-increasing desire led me to attend a youth camp a few months after my sixteenth birthday. I had heard my grandparents share the joy and beauty of their spiritual experiences, and I often listened as my father or other men of God preached on the baptism of the Holy Spirit. They expounded the Scriptures, explaining that a believer must be a witness for Jesus and that to be an effective witness one must receive the fullness of the Holy Spirit. I knew that I needed His anointing in my life if I was going to do anything of eternal value. So, I was hungry for God and wanted desperately to be used by God for His glory. The hunger to know God had emerged like slow-rising dough.

Hungry for His Presence

After four years of missionary service in India, our family had returned to the United States for a year of itineration. The deep desire within me for more of God and the fullness of His Spirit had increased. So, when I heard about a youth camp that was to be held in a small community of West Virginia, I asked to attend. The camp had been built many years before. The main center for campers to gather for worship was an old-fashioned tabernacle with long, hard pews and wooden altar railings that stretched across the front of the platform.

One night, the camp evangelist preached on the baptism of the Holy Spirit. I don't remember anything that he said. I just know that as he preached, the hunger for God grew stronger in my heart. When he finally stopped preaching, he invited those who were seeking the baptism of the Holy Spirit to come forward for prayer.

At the evangelist's invitation, I hobbled forward, leaning heavily on the crutches that I was using as a result of the cut on my foot. When I got to the front, I laid aside my crutches and began to pray fervently, seeking the Lord, pleading with Him earnestly to fill me with His Holy Spirit.

More than two hours passed as I continued praying. In fact, I would have grown weary except for two reasons—first, two girls were praying with me and for me. They were full of joy and excitement, and their elation compelled me to continue seeking God for the blessing that they had experienced; second, I was deeply hungry and believed the promises of Jesus when He said, *"Ask, and it will be given to you; seek, and you will find."*[38] He also said, *"Blessed are those who hunger and thirst for righteousness, for they shall be satisfied."*[39] I believed those promises and trusted them that night as time passed in fervent, pleading prayer.

After a couple of hours had passed, I prayed, "Jesus, I have done everything I know to do. I have praised You. I have knelt down, stood up, and raised my hands. I have done everything I know how to do to yield to Your Spirit. Now, You will have to do it."

Suddenly, just as those words passed through my mind and over my lips, I felt an overwhelming sense of the presence of God. A moment later, I was speaking in tongues ecstatically and joyfully basking in the wonderful presence of God. I was filled with the Holy Spirit.

That experience opened the door to a deeper spiritual walk with God. A blessed assurance of salvation and a steadfast faith that God was with me engulfed me. Further, I immediately felt a great urge to tell someone about Jesus.

Moses was prepared to stand before Pharaoh with the authority of God, yet there was one more important

38. Matthew 7:7
39. Matthew 5:6

lesson that Moses was required to take before he could walk into Egypt and Pharaoh's presence as a voice for God and His people.

Chapter 9

Is There Anything You Are Holding Back?

"A baseball player who expects to excel in the game without adequate exercise of his body is no more ridiculous than the Christian who hopes to be able to act in the manner of Christ when put to the test without the appropriate exercise in godly living."
— Dallas Willard[40]

Now it came about at the lodging place on the way that the Lord met him and sought to put him to death. Then Zipporah took a flint and cut off her son's foreskin and threw it at Moses' feet, and she said, "You are indeed a bridegroom of blood to me." So He let him alone. At that

40. Dallas Willard, The Spirit of the Disciplines: Understanding How God Changes Lives (San Francisco: Harper & Row, 1988), 4.

time she said, "You are a bridegroom of blood"—because of the circumcision.[41]

Can two walk together, except they be agreed?[42]

Moses was eager to return to Egypt. He began the long journey back with the vision and voice of God still fresh in his heart and mind. He was full of excitement and urgency as he hurried toward Egypt, retracing the steps through the hot desert sands that he had traveled years before when he was a frightened fugitive scurrying for his life. The vision of leadership that he once carried as a young man in Egypt of leading his people out of slavery had again been restored through his discourse with God at the burning bush. The staff in his hand was a reminder that God was with him and that God would help him.

Moses broke his journey for a night of rest at a lodging place along the way. There, God taught him the secret of continued anointing and a lifetime of living in the presence of God.

The conversation that God and Moses had that night at the lodging place is not recorded in Scripture, but we know the gist of what was said and we see the results of the encounter. It was foundational for what God was going to do when Moses returned to Egypt,

---

41. Exodus 4:24-26
42. Amos 3:3, KJV

but it was equally important, if not more so, to what God would do on Mount Sinai.

Moses had married Zipporah, the daughter of Reuel, and God had given them a son. Moses had probably tried to circumcise his son according to the covenant established with Abraham, but Zipporah thought that circumcision was a strange and dirty custom. She must have expressed her disgust and may have even refused to allow such a thing to be done to her son. Moses ceded his convictions in the face of his wife's confrontation.

That night, at the lodging place on the road from Midian to Egypt, God met Moses. He did not meet him with good news or with a comforting word of assurance. God met Moses with a threat to kill him for his disobedience.

Moses knew God's will and expectations, but he chose to side with his wife to keep peace in the family. He compromised the known will of God for the sake of convenience and acceptance. Instead of circumcising his son, he acquiesced to the desires of his wife in order to please her.

The desire to please one's spouse is usually good and most often contributes to a healthy marriage. Dialogue and negotiation are essential ingredients in marriage; however, it is never healthy or wise to compromise on biblical principles and commands.

Hungry for His Presence

Relationships within families and churches that respect God's commands are the healthiest.

Obedience is a key ingredient in the life of the person who wishes to experience the presence of God. Moses had been called by God to lead the children of Israel out of Egypt. Moses had been equipped with powerful gifts, but there was still one key ingredient missing—obedience.

Moses knew what God demanded but had not obeyed Him. Consequently, God would not allow him to go any further until he obeyed. There, at the lodging place with the stark cost of rebellion confronting him, Moses finally obeyed God and circumcised his son.

Once Moses obeyed, the blessings of God rested on him. The Spirit of God led him, and the power of God was evidenced through him. Obedience was essential to Moses' ministry, message, and mission.

Do you wonder why your ministry is ineffective? Does your message not resonate with the congregation or audience? Now, be honest. Is there any area of disobedience in your life? If so, let it go. Turn from your sin, and obey God's command to you; otherwise, you will die in your disobedience—perhaps not physically, but spiritually and emotionally you *will* die. The presence of God will withdraw from you, and you will die.

I have a friend in the ministry, Mohan C. Lazarus, whom I have grown to love and respect. God has used him powerfully. Many thousands have been saved, untold numbers miraculously healed, and multitudes delivered from demonic bondage as a result of God's power and presence in his ministry.

People have often asked him, "Why does God use you so powerfully?" His simple answer is, "I try to do everything Jesus tells me to do." That is obedience—and God blesses obedience.

You can expect to find God's presence in the place where His people are living lives of obedience.

Chapter 10

Do You Have Challenges Facing You?

Moses did not return to Egypt to simply fulfill his dreams and personal ambitions. He returned to Egypt by the command of God and as an instrument of God to fulfill God's purposes; in doing so, however, Moses fulfilled the designs and purposes that had been seeded into his life at an early age. When he learned to recognize and honor God's presence, his calling became apparent to everyone. Moses accomplished God's design for his life.

When we learn to honor and obey God in every area of our lives, the door is opened for God to use us and to make His name great through us. We can never fulfill our divine destiny and purpose until we first learn to respect and obey the One who designed, formed, and made us.

The lessons Moses had learned and the promises that he had received became foundational to his usefulness in God's hands. God was with Moses, and everyone recognized it. Moses first left Egypt as a renegade and a convicted criminal, but he returned as a servant of the Most High God and as His spokesman.

Moses was a servant of God; yet, his life and ministry in Egypt were not without problems and difficulties. His faith and his obedience would be tested through conflicts with his own people and threats from Pharaoh. Those difficulties would further teach Moses to trust God and depend on His presence.

Sometimes, when we begin to walk and live in the presence of God, people will become skeptical and question our integrity and motivation. Such was the case for Moses. He arrived in Egypt with a flourish and was at first received by the elders of the sons of Israel with much excitement.

> *Then Moses and Aaron went and assembled all the elders of the sons of Israel; and Aaron spoke all the words which the Lord had spoken to Moses. He then performed the signs in the sight of the people. So the people believed; and when they heard that the Lord was concerned about the sons of Israel and that He had seen their affliction, then they bowed low and worshiped.*[43]

43. Exodus 4:29-31

David Stewart

Everything seemed to be going according to plan and in the way Moses had envisioned it, but soon his plans began to fall apart. He went to Pharaoh demanding that he release God's people. In response, Pharaoh refused and ordered that the Israelite people be treated more cruelly and harshly than before.

When the new demands were made on the Israelites, they assaulted Moses with angry words. The elders said, "May the Lord look upon you and judge you, for you have made us odious in Pharaoh's sight and in the sight of his servants, to put a sword in their hand to kill us."[44] The people were no longer impressed by Moses' claims or the miraculous works that he performed with his staff.

The old doubts began to surface. Moses questioned his qualifications and capabilities. He reminded God of his inability to convincingly speak. Moses had arrived in Egypt full of confidence and enthusiasm, but his desire and will began to wane.

There was one important difference—God was with Moses. Because of that, God reassured him of His plans for His people and His purposes for Moses' life. Once again, doubts dissipated and faith began to rise.

God's presence does not guarantee a trouble-free existence or a carefree life, but it does ensure that when difficulties or problems arise, we have His strength, power, and wisdom to lead and assist us.

44. Exodus 5:21

Hungry for His Presence

The Word of God assures us in Psalms 91:1-9:

He who dwells in the shelter of the Most High
Will abide in the shadow of the Almighty.
I will say to the Lord, "My refuge and my fortress,
My God, in whom I trust!"
For it is He who delivers you from the snare
of the trapper
And from the deadly pestilence.
He will cover you with His pinions,
And under His wings you may seek refuge;
His faithfulness is a shield and bulwark.

You will not be afraid of the terror by night,
Or of the arrow that flies by day;
Of the pestilence that stalks in darkness,
Or of the destruction that lays waste at noon.
A thousand may fall at your side
And ten thousand at your right hand,
But it shall not approach you.
You will only look on with your eyes
And see the recompense of the wicked.
For you have made the Lord, my refuge,
Even the Most High, your dwelling place.

Chapter 11

Are You Willing to Follow His Direction?

The Lord was going before them in a pillar of cloud by day to lead them on the way, and in a pillar of fire by night to give them light, that they might travel by day and by night.[45]

After many trials and tests, signs and wonders, and manifestations of the favor of God upon Moses and the Israelites, Pharaoh relented and released the people. They were free to go—but where? What direction would they take?

Moses had first met God at a burning bush in the wilderness. He had learned to recognize the voice of God, to honor and obey Him, and to trust His leading as a result of that experience. Now, God would lead Moses through the wilderness by a pillar of cloud during the day and a fire by night.

45. Exodus 13:21

Hungry for His Presence

Once again, Moses would need to honor and obey God. His life and the lives of all the people depended on God's presence and on Moses' ability and willingness to boldly follow God's directives. They moved when the cloud moved and remained still when the pillar rested.

God's people must similarly learn to live in God's presence and depend on His constant leadership and direction. Without the presence of God, churches will find themselves wandering through dry and barren places. They can dream big, set ambitious goals, and cast captivating vision, but if God is not leading they are just meandering aimlessly without real purpose or meaning.

Some years ago, I was encouraged to attend a vision-casting and planning meeting for leaders engaged in a variety of different ministries. During the course of several days of meetings, there were presentations, group discussions, and robust debate. On the last day of our gathering, innovative policy statements and purpose-driven directives were presented. The attending delegates were challenged to consider ways of implementing the new strategies that had been advocated.

As I look back on that meeting and reflect on our time together, I find one lingering memory that left the deepest impression. The meetings opened with a brief devotional thought and a very short prayer. The meditation and prayer seemed obligatory, as if offered for those in attendance who were "old school." This portion had the feel of disregarded items on an agenda that needed to be disposed of as quickly as possible. I left with a deep sense of sorrow.

Churches place great emphasis on annual business meetings, monthly board meetings, and weekly staff meetings. Some people—who rarely darken the church doors otherwise—go through great effort to attend these meetings. Members who neither have a ministry nor would ever witness to a friend or neighbor stand and vehemently argue over numbers, rules, and ideas. Some are willing to cause dissension and division in the body over mundane and carnal matters that have no bearing on men's eternal condition or spiritual needs.

The early church had leadership and congregational meetings, but their meetings were characterized by intense times of prayer and seeking the face of the Lord.

The book of Acts records several occasions in which the church was challenged by contemporary problems that it faced. Several issues had the potential to disrupt or destroy the work of God. In each case, however, through prayer and fasting church leaders found the answers that benefited the church and facilitated the spreading of the gospel. Acts 15 records one of the greatest conflicts that the early church faced. There was debate as to whether Gentiles should be included in the church and whether Jewish people should take the gospel to Gentiles. They engaged one another in robust debate, with strong feelings on both sides of the issue. Finally, through prayer and a sense of the presence of God, the leaders came to an agreement. They characterized their agreement in the letter that was to be sent to all the churches. Verse 28 summarizes their meeting, *"For it seemed good to the Holy Spirit and to us."*[46] The presence of God made the difference in the meetings and directed all of their decisions.

Am I suggesting that we do away with discussion, debate, or deliberation? No! I am, however, strongly advocating, advising, and encouraging that prayer be considered our highest order of business. We must wait on God, invite His presence to come, and allow the Holy Spirit to lead us in our deliberations. Waiting on God and inviting His presence must become a priority rather than mere protocol. It should be the main order of business rather than an item on the agenda.

We need the presence of God in our meetings, not only on Sunday morning but also in our business and leadership meetings. When we have the presence of God, we will be assured of the direction of God.

God's leading is evidenced in the following verses:

> *God led the people.*[47]

---

46. Acts 15:28
47. Exodus 13:18

David Stewart

You shall remember all the way which the Lord your God has led you in the wilderness.[48]

He led you through the great and terrible wilderness.[49]

I have led you forty years.[50]

Our Lord Jesus understood the importance of living daily in the presence of God. He was constantly aware of and obedient to the Spirit's direction. Luke 4:1 tells us, *"Jesus, full of the Holy Spirit, returned from the Jordan and was led around by the Spirit in the wilderness."*

Moses and the people of Israel not only escaped Egypt, but by God's direction and ever-present power the Egyptians were defeated and left dead in the Red Sea. Just as Moses was dependent on God and His presence, so we must be totally reliant on Him in every decision.

---

49. Deuteronomy 8:15
50. Deuteronomy 29:5

Chapter 12

Do You Want Him More Than Anything?

"All who have walked with God have
viewed prayer as the main business
of their lives."
— Richard Foster[51]

*My presence shall go with you, and I
will give you rest.*[52]

When the people of Israel left Egypt and
Egyptian slavery, they passed through
the Red Sea and began to make their way
through the wilderness to the Promised Land. God
led them. As discussed in the previous chapter, He did
so by manifesting Himself and his guiding presence
through a pillar of cloud by day and a pillar of fire by
night. Exodus 13:22 reads, *"He did not take away the*

---

51. Foster, *Celebration*, 34.
52. Exodus 33:14

pillar of cloud by day, nor the pillar of fire by night, from before the people." They were constantly aware that God was leading them.

Then, the people of Israel sinned by making a golden calf. They worshiped the golden calf and proclaimed it was a god who had led them out of Egypt. The Almighty God was offended.

In spite of the people's wickedness, God told Moses to take the rebellious people into the land that He had promised them and their forefather Abraham. He would not break His promise. He would even send an angel before them to guide them, but He would not go with them. He said to Moses, *"I will not go up in your midst."*[53]

Those words frightened Moses. He was desperate for God's direction and help. The leadership task that he had been given was great, and he felt inadequate for the work that he was called to do without the presence of God.

When God spoke to Moses that day, Moses knew that God was angry. He thought that many of the people would die or be left behind because of their sin. Thus, he wanted to know whom he was to lead and where he was to lead them.

Moses pleaded for God's assistance and direction. More importantly, Moses also reminded God that He had

---

53. Exodus 33:3

claimed that Israel was His own. The implication was, "How can You leave us alone? How can You forsake us?"

In response to Moses' plea, God promised His abiding presence. He said, *"My presence shall go with you."* God continued to lead the people by the pillar by day and the fire by night. Whenever the cloud moved, the people moved. When the cloud stopped the people halted.

This story teaches us that the presence of God provides direction for our lives. He is the source of guidance, direction, and wisdom. Without Him, we are lost and wander aimlessly through life.

We often seek direction from our own minds when we should follow the direction of the Spirit. The book of Acts reminds us of the importance of seeking God's Spirit for direction. The scripture reads, *"For it seemed good to the Holy Spirit and to us."*[54] The New Testament believers made decisions based on God's directives and commands. They looked to the leadership of the Holy Spirit for focus and direction for their lives.

Costly mistakes are made when leaders place an inordinate amount of emphasis on developing and casting vision without first consulting the leadership and direction of the Spirit. Church leaders ought to put emphasis on seeking the Lord and following His directions. He knows the way ahead; He knows the obstacles we will face; He knows the strategy required

54. Acts 15:28

to defeat the enemy and the methods needed to enter into the Promised Land.

Organizations conduct development and strategic planning sessions with little consideration of the Spirit's leading. They have ministry mapping events and team building exercises, but they do not actively invite and ardently pursue the presence of God in those meetings.

Meetings are opened with a perfunctory prayer. Then, participants proceed to share ideas and thoughts without further consideration of God's holy presence. Meetings are held in the name of God but are conducted without honoring God.

Moses' life story reminds us again and again that direction comes from the voice and presence of God. Not only does Moses' life illustrate this truth, but other stories throughout Scripture exemplify men and women who sought the presence of God when faced with important decisions.

In the book of Acts, we find that Peter was fasting and praying when he received the God-given vision and directions to go to Cornelius' house. This changed the face of ministry for the early church. Gentiles would be reached with the Gospel.

In another instance in the book of Acts, the Spirit forbade Paul from ministering in Asia. While he was praying and seeking God, God gave him a vision of a Macedonian man calling him. This further gave direction and momentum to the preaching of the gospel to Gentile people and nations.

Furthermore, the Lord Jesus Himself sought direction while in the presence of God during prayer. Before His ministry began, Jesus went into the wilderness for an extended time of fasting and prayer. Before He called and appointed the twelve disciples, He spent all night praying and seeking the direction of the Father. Then, just before His crucifixion, Jesus spent agonizing hours in the garden of Gethsemane drawing strength from the presence of God.

The Scripture says, *"The steps of a good man are ordered by the Lord."*[55] Moses did not want to make the journey or lead the people alone. He knew the task was so daunting that it would crush him if he were to try to lead the people with his own skill and intellect.

Moses understood that the way would be filled with hardship and difficult decisions, but he also understood that he could endure suffering and hardship when God's presence was near. When we have God's presence, there is a calm assurance that we can tolerate any suffering and hardship that we may face.

Moses would face difficult situations en route to the Promised Land, but because God's presence was near he had great courage. He possessed the assurance that

55. Psalm 37:23, KJV

Hungry for His Presence

God could bring water out of the rock when there was no water to be found. Moses faced potential famine conditions, but he understood that God was able to cause manna to fall from heaven.

Moses was unafraid to face kings, armies, and giants when he knew that God was with him. Because Moses had seen God destroy Pharaoh and his armies in the Red Sea, he had the assurance that God would defeat the kings who opposed him, the giants who tried to stop him, and the armies that tried to conquer him.

Do we attempt to lead a congregation or ministry without prayer or a constant awareness of His presence? This type of carnal leadership has devastating effects on a church and on the work of God. A church may grow and have numerical success, but without the presence of God, defeat and destruction are not far away.

When we have the assurance of His presence we can also face armies, giants, and kings. We can live with confidence that God will give us the victory. God's presence is the assurance of strength and power in our lives.

God told Moses, *"My presence shall go with you."*[56] That was wonderful, yet more wonderful still, in the fortieth chapter of Exodus we find that God chose to have a dwelling place among His people.

---

56. Exodus 33:14

David Stewart

He was with them; His presence abode among them. His glory was evident. He was not only leading them; He was in their very midst.

You can expect the very same thing. His presence will be the thing that sets you and your church apart from other people and other churches. Do you want His presence more than anything else?

Chapter 13

How Do I Experience His Presence?

"In the midst of an exceedingly
busy ministry Jesus made a habit of
withdrawing to 'a lonely place apart'
(Matt. 14:13). He did this not just to
be away from people, but so he could
be with God."
— Richard Foster[57]

O ur modern society seems to be in an ever-
increasing frenzy to accomplish more goals,
and do everything faster. We are in a hurry,
and I think God wants to help us slow down. He
wants us to value our relationship with Him so
deeply that we will give Him our most precious
commodity—our time.

Slow down. Don't be in such a hurry. We rush our
phone calls. We send short texts. We message others

57. Foster, *Celebration*, 16.

in bite size segments of 140 letters or less. Don't let the rush of daily life dictate the pace of your spiritual life.

Next, settle yourself. Calm down. Turn off the engines that drive you from one event to another, from conversation to conversation, and from one relationship to another.

Disengage yourself by choosing to sit at His feet, offering your praises and worship to Him. Sing a song (or songs) of surrender, adoration, or simple praise. Whisper His name. Just smile into His loving face.

Now, begin your conversation with Him. Express yourself to Him clearly, frankly, and honestly. He is a very good listener. He usually waits quietly while we pour our hearts out to Him.

He likes to hear His children's voices. So, talk to Him. Tell Him your needs, fears, and desires, and ask the questions that fill your heart and mind. He is not intimidated by your questions. Ask Him to reveal His plans, His direction, and His will to you.

Then, He expects us to wait for His answer—His words to us. He is never in a hurry and may be offended when we are too hurried to wait for His still small voice.

> *Yet those who wait for the Lord will gain new strength; they will mount up with wings like eagles, they will run and*

*not get tired, they will walk and not
become weary.*[58]

*I waited patiently for the Lord; and He
inclined to me and heard my cry.*[59]

Wait patiently for the Lord and He will answer you.

As you wait, expect Him to speak. He is pleased with
such simple, child-like faith. Don't jabber on and on.
It may be proof that you are not expectant. Wait with
faith and hope. Wait silently.

He will speak to you.

I have found that when he speaks His words are so
powerful that just one word can transform me. When
He speaks to me He does not usually say much;
however, it is powerful, thrilling, and life changing.

Many years ago I spent a few days in fasting and prayer.
I had chosen to spend the time secluded away from
family, friends, and ministry team members. The room
I was staying in contained two double beds, a desk,
and a chair. My Bible, a notebook, and a couple of other
devotional books were the only things that I took with
me, besides a few articles of clothing and personal items.

There was no particular problem or specific question
for which I was seeking an answer. There was no
urgent need. I just wanted to be in His presence.

---

58. Isaiah 40:31
59. Psalms 40:1

Hungry for His Presence

As I have often done, I interspersed Bible reading and meditation with times of worship and prayer. My Scripture meditations were taken from the Gospel of John.

In the afternoon of the third and final day of my fast, I began to feel a little fatigued—probably the effects of low blood sugar. So, I moved to the bed, lay down, and tried to take a short nap, but I was not sleepy.

As I lay quietly on the bed with my eyes open, I spoke out loud saying, "Father, is there anything You want to say to me?"

His answer came suddenly and clearly. "I love you."

That was all: "I love you."

There was no audible voice, but it was as clear in my spirit as I have ever heard anyone's voice in my physical ears. "I love you."

In the next moment, I sat upright on the bed. My feet hit the floor, and I moved quickly to the desk. Opening my Bible, I looked down at the page to which I turned, and I read the following passage:

> *Jesus answered and said to him, "If anyone loves Me, he will keep My word; and My Father will love him, and We will come to him and make Our abode with him."*[60]

60. John 14:23

David Stewart

My heart was overwhelmed. Over and over again, I said, "He loves me. He loves me," as tears of joy flowed freely down my cheeks. "He loves me. He loves me. The Father loves me."

Quiet yourself. He is present—omnipresent. You don't have to wait for Him to come. He is present. He waits for you; He waits for you to seek, honor, and enjoy His presence.

One of the ways that we can quiet ourselves before God is through the faithful practice of setting aside a day for Sabbath worship. A few years ago, after a prolonged period of continued travel and ministry, I became emotionally and physically exhausted and found myself on the verge of emotional and physical collapse. A few days afterward, during a time of devotion, the Lord spoke to me very clearly and strongly about honoring the Sabbath. At first, I felt confused; I thought that I had honored the Sabbath all my life by faithfully attending church every Sunday. Then, as I studied the Scriptures I realized that the Sabbath was not simply a commandment to attend church. The commandment to honor the Sabbath is a commandment to rest from work and pursue fellowship with God in His presence.

The Lord convicted me that I had tried to obey all the Ten Commandments except for this one commandment. Asking God to forgive me, I immediately implemented a Sabbath rest in my life. That practice has enhanced and blessed my life in innumerable ways. Psalms

Hungry for His Presence

131:2 states, *"Surely I have composed and quieted my soul; like a weaned child rests against his mother, my soul is like a weaned child within me."*

Wait! I say it again. Wait! Wait on the Lord.

Chapter 14

How Do We Experience His Presence Together?

"Though we come to an event where He is the Guest of Honor, it is possible to give Him a routine gift, sing a few customary songs to Him, and then totally neglect Him while we focus on others and enjoy the performance of those in front of us."
— Donald Whitney[61]

First, turn off the hype. God is not a rock star who has come to entertain us. He is not a professional wrestler who feeds off of surging, manic energy. God does not need loud excited carnival barkers to entice people into His tent, nor does He need performers who have mastered the art of drama to move people to a

61. Donald S. Whitney, *Spiritual Disciplines for the Christian Life* (Colorado Springs: Navpress, 1991), 86.

point of decision. No! God is not impressed by our fleshly exhibitions of emotional manipulation in the name of religious celebration.

God doesn't need the hype, melodramatic presentations, or high-pressure sales technique that we might think He does. We are so used to glamour and glitz, pumping bass and pounding bongos, dancers, flashing lights, and entertainers that if we don't have them we get bored quickly. We crave emotional caffeine.

Don't misunderstand me. Our ministry team has often used lights, big sound systems, and has tried to produce ministry with high quality and standards. Furthermore, I have often felt a surge of emotion and fervor when preaching the gospel. Excellence and enthusiasm in ministry are important; however, the point I am making is that God doesn't need or require sensationalism or actors performing to stir people's emotional response.

He is the Ruler of the universe, the Lord of All, the Almighty One, and the Mighty Creator. God is, and there is none beside Him. He made the moon, the sun, and the stars. He spoke the worlds into existence and formed man with His own hands. He breathed life into man and watched as Adam stood and took his first step. When we invite Him into a service, His presence and His Word can stop men in their tracks, turn them around, and set them on a life-altering path.

Our skilled, finely tuned, and timed productions may betray a lack of faith in the miraculous, majestic worth of God. We think that we have to do something spectacular to get people to come. We forget that Jesus said, *"And I, if I am lifted up from the earth, will draw all men to Myself."*[62] We don't need hype to draw the presence of God or entice people. We need Jesus. Stop the drama—the play-acting. Turn off the hype.

Second, turn the attention away from man. So much of what is done in church is man-centered, glorifying man's skills, achievements, and accomplishments. We turn worship leaders into stars, pastors into CEOs, and congregants into pampered, spoiled fans who hop from one venue to the next.

Much of what we do is focused on a man or woman and his or her talent or gift. When a song is sung, we applaud the performer. Preachers boast in their efforts saying, "I am preaching better than you are responding."

It often feels like church is just another show—an entertaining performance. It becomes a show of the flesh because the focus is on man's efforts and needs. We mention God, but the focus of our music is on the skills of the musicians, the vocal abilities of the singers, and the musical tastes of people whom we are trying to attract. The focus of our preaching is on what will make us healthier, wealthier, or wiser.

---

62. John 12:32

We even give our resources with the hope of spoken promises that it will be returned to us tenfold or a hundredfold.

Are we seeking the glory that belongs to Him? Beware. He destroys the arrogant and proud. He brings down the haughty, but He lifts up those who seek the glory and honor of God. God says, *"For My own sake, for My own sake, I will act; for how can My name be profaned? And My glory I will not give to another."*[63]

In the early days of my ministry, God spoke clearly and powerfully to me on two separate occasions through two of His dear servants. One who spoke God's word to me was a woman evangelist and prophetess; the other was the pastor of a very large church.

The instruction from the Lord was very similar in both instances. "Son, you must always be very careful to give Me glory and honor for everything that I do through you. If you honor me, I will bless your ministry." Those words have remained with me throughout the years, serving as both an encouragement and a warning to me.

The challenge that we face is to find methods of using people's gifts, talents, and callings without taking the focus away from our Savior, Lord, and King. We must learn how to lead passionate worship services; offer heartfelt, even emotional prayers; and preach powerful, effective messages without evoking undue

63. Isaiah 48:11

David Stewart

honor or attention for ourselves. We must turn the attention away from man.

Third, in order for us to corporately experience the presence of God we must turn our eyes and hearts toward Jesus. This is one of the surest ways to experience the presence of God. Look to Jesus!

When I was in the second grade, my parents put me into a boarding school for my studies. My parents only came to visit once or twice a semester, but my mom wrote me two letters weekly. She ended each of her letters with the simple words, "Keep your eyes on Jesus."

Hebrews 12:2 gives us clear instruction, admonishing us to "[look] unto Jesus the author and finisher of our faith; who for the joy that was set before him endured the cross, despising the shame, and is set down at the right hand of the throne of God."[64]

If we want to truly experience the presence of God, we must ask ourselves a few questions. The first is, "Do we revere the Lord?"

God spoke to Moses, saying, *"You shall keep My Sabbaths and reverence My sanctuary; I am the Lord."*[65] God is in essence saying, "Do not forget who I am. When you come to Me, you must treat Me with fear, respect, and awe."

64. KJV
65. Leviticus 26:2

Hungry for His Presence

The important question that must be asked is, "Do we revere the Lord?" To revere Him is to show Him the honor and respect that He deserves.

As was mentioned in Chapter 3, priests, police, and political leaders were once considered worthy of special honor. Doctors, professors, and teachers were respected and admired. Yet, today, with the cultural shift to egalitarian thinking, these professions are no longer favored, nor are they given special privileges or rank within society.

Sadly, this cultural trend is reflected in worship services. People approach God as if He were a colleague, a neighbor, or a carnal lover. The fear, awe, and respect that are due the Almighty God are missing.

Church services are treated like religious rock festivals. Sometimes, I am reminded of the heathen practices of the children of Israel when Aaron had fashioned a golden calf for them to worship. They sang, danced, and worshiped, but their behavior reflected pagan worship of the day, dishonored God, and deeply offended Him.

Do we reverence God when we enter church? Do we reverence God when we sing, give in the offering, pray, or preach? Do we reverence Him when we turn to greet one another or interact with one another during the worship service? If we want to experience the presence of God, we cannot afford to dishonor or disrespect our Lord through any irreverence.

Approach Him with awe and fear. He is the Omnipotent One, the Omniscient One, and the Omnipresent One. He is greater than the President—would you not show the President more respect than we give God on an average Sunday morning?

When we enter church, let us encourage one another to recognize that we have come to worship. Refrain from foolish joking, conversation that distracts our attention from looking to Jesus, or anything that sidetracks us from our call to worship.

Reverence the Lord.

The second question that we should ask ourselves in order to enjoy the presence of God as a corporate body is, "Do we obey God?" Obedience is revealed in both our practices and our attitudes.

Our Lord Jesus said, "He who has My commandments and keeps them is the one who loves Me."[66] He went on to say, "If anyone loves Me, he will keep My word."[67]

Do we obey God? It is clear—people who are devotees and disciples of Jesus will obey His Word. They choose to live in obedience to God's Word because they love Jesus.

It is no wonder that the presence of God is not sensed in some churches when a few members who are self-professed followers of Jesus are living

---

66. John 14:21
67. John 14:23

in disobedience to God's Word. They flaunt their lifestyles, exuding arrogance as they demand not to be judged.

We believe that the power of Jesus is transformative, yet there are church members, worship team leaders, and others who are given leadership or ministry roles openly living in disobedience to God's Word. This is offensive to God and robs entire congregations of the opportunity to experience His presence.

God expects His children to reflect His righteousness. He calls His people to holiness, saying, "For I am the Lord who brought you up from the land of Egypt to be your God; thus you shall be holy, for I am holy."[68]

In our desire to follow Christ and experience His presence, we must willingly choose to forsake all sexual promiscuity, pornography, gambling, drunkenness, lying, and cheating, as they are behaviors that God condemns. His children are not to indulge themselves in such self-gratifying ways. These things must grieve our Lord and, in doing so, keep us from the true longing of our hearts—to please and obey Him.

Do our attitudes reflect hearts of surrender and obedience to God? Worshipers must be careful lest their desire for self-expression and their cultural biases cause them to commit willful disobedience to God's Word. While God does not specify what we

68. Leviticus 11:45

should wear, His Word does command that women dress modestly and that men are in attire that reflect the values in God's Word.

Our attitudes are sometimes reflected in the way we approach God in worship. Paul told the Corinthian believers, "*If anyone is hungry, let him eat at home, so that you will not come together for judgment.*"[69] Yet, there is a church culture that invites worshipers to bring coffee, doughnuts, and other refreshments into the house of worship. Even if such behavior is not a form of direct disobedience to Paul's teaching, perhaps we should at least ask ourselves, "Are we guilty of disrespect and casualness that is not conducive to entertaining the presence of God?" Would we visit the Oval Office with a cup of coffee and a donut in hand? Is it not sinful to show less respect to God than we would to a national leader?

Racism and classism are still rampant in many churches today. Some churches do not welcome people of a different skin color, language, or nationality. These things are surely offensive to God because He says, "*For God is the King of all the earth.*"[70] Furthermore, He says that He desires for all people to be saved.[71]

---

69. 1 Corinthians 11:34

70. Psalms 47:7

71. See 1 Timothy 2:3-4.

Hungry for His Presence

Bitterness is a scourge in many churches and Christian fellowships. Anger over trivial issues often leads to division and to bitterness. Jesus demanded that His followers forgive one another. He said:

> *For if you forgive others for their transgressions, your heavenly Father will also forgive you. But if you do not forgive others, then your Father will not forgive your transgressions.*[72]

If we are going to enjoy the presence of God corporately, we are all responsible to live in obedience to God's Word.

The third question that must be asked if we are to experience the presence of God when we gather together is, "Do we love God?"

God called Moses up the mountain to meet with Him. From the mountaintop, God gave Moses the Ten Commandments and the Law. God was making a covenant with His people. He was not merely offering them a legal contract to co-exist; He was calling them to a love relationship much like a marriage.

John talks about the relationship of Jesus and the church in similar terms in the book of Revelation:

> *Let us rejoice and be glad and give the glory to Him, for the marriage of the*

72. Matthew 6:14-15

Lamb has come and His bride has made herself ready.[73]

Then one of the seven angels who had the seven bowls full of the seven last plagues came and spoke with me, saying, "Come here, I will show you the bride, the wife of the Lamb."[74]

The church is called to a love relationship with Jesus. He is grieved when we treat our relationship with Him like a legal contract between business partners or like the relationship that citizens have with a national government.

Is Jesus preeminent in our lives? Do we acknowledge and respect Him like Paul says a wife should her husband? Do we long to spend time in His presence? Do we love Him?

---

73. Revelation 19:7
74. Revelation 21:9

Chapter 15

Will You Take Time to Pray?

Worship has been an important part of my personal life and public ministry. A few years ago, my ministry team and I led two different worship services that were recorded on video. Thousands of people attended each event and testified that the gatherings were a great blessing to them; many thousands more have enjoyed the videos that were released.

Not only have I emphasized worship in my ministry, but also, for many years now, worship has been a priority of the Evangelical, Pentecostal, and Charismatic church world. Worship, as an experience and a lifestyle, has been emphasized and promoted. Worship celebration services, worship seminars, and worship music have become popular and part of contemporary church culture.

The previous season of church history called for an emphasis on worship. The church needed to learn to worship freely and exuberantly, and God graciously created that desire in the hearts of His people. Believers who were thirsty longed for the quenching river of the Spirit that flows during corporate worship, but now there is a new season that the Spirit is calling for.

Today, the church must continue to worship, but it must move forward through the outer gates of praise and beyond the courts of worship to enter the holy place of sacrifice and step into the holy place where intercession is made. The church must learn to pray.

Christians in the last century often spent long intervals in fervent prayer. Pentecostal pioneers taught and practiced tarrying—extended prayer times. Their tarrying services sometimes lasted through the night as they waited on God in prayer with the hopes that they would be filled with the Holy Spirit. Those fathers and mothers of faith spent many hours in personal prayer closets, around church altar benches, and in sawdust-filled tabernacles crying out to God for personal revival and for community wide renewal and awakening— and God answered their prayers.

The Bible records several stories of leaders who called the people to prayer during times of national crisis. Esther called the people for prayer during a time of danger.[75] Hezekiah called the people to prayer

---

75. See Esther 4:16.

David Stewart

during a time of national repentance.[76] Nehemiah called the people to prayer during a time of rebuilding and revival.[77]

When the people prayed, God answered as He had promised to do. God had spoken to Solomon. Saying:

> *If I shut up the heavens so that there is no rain, or if I command the locust to devour the land, or if I send pestilence among My people, and My people who are called by My name humble themselves and pray and seek My face and turn from their wicked ways, then I will hear from heaven, will forgive their sin and will heal their land.*[78]

It is time today for the church to rise up and pray. The need of the nations calls for it. The lost cry out for it. The lukewarm condition of the church demands it. It is time to pray.

Let us cry out before the Father until our hearts are fully committed and surrendered to His will and His call. Let us cry out until His passion for the lost stirs us to move beyond the comfort of an easy lifestyle to the commitment of sacrificial living and giving. Let us pray until God graciously creates a hunger for His

76. See 2 Chronicles 30.
77. See Nehemiah 9:1-2.
78. 2 Chronicles 7:13-14

presence in the hearts of His people wherever they may meet or gather.

God is raising up a prayer movement in the western church. Followers of Christ in North America and Europe will join hands with believers from around the world who intercede for the nations. Their voices have been raised on behalf of the spiritually lost. It is time for us to join them in fervent prayer.

Let us pray until we hear from heaven and He heals our land. Let us pray until we are sick of sin and hungry for holiness, until we are weary of sensual pleasure and endless hours of foolish entertainment and are only satisfied with the Spirit's fullness and the joy of His presence. Let us pray until we groan for the lost and rejoice to see the salvation of perishing men and women, until His presence fills our hearts, our houses of worship, our homes, and our nation.

A few years ago, after we had been called to lead our congregation here in Leominster, Massachusetts, the Holy Spirit led me to do several key things regarding prayer. First, the Holy Spirit prompted me to invite others into my private morning devotional time. This was something I had never done before, but I felt that my example in prayer could cause others to pray and create a hunger in their hearts.

So, I invited a man (who has since become a deacon on our church council) to join me for prayer at 7:30 a.m. in our church sanctuary. He agreed and we began meeting, seeking the face of God. We prayed asking Him for an outpouring of His Spirit in our church.

After we had been praying together for a few weeks, I asked him if he knew of someone who might like to join us. He did, and shortly thereafter, a man and his wife began joining us for prayer. They have been faithfully attending that morning prayer time for more than two years.

Slowly others joined with us for this blessed time of personal worship and intercession. The church is usually opened at 7:30 a.m. and prayer continues till 9:30 a.m. Throughout the morning different ones join us—some for ten minutes and others for an hour or more. Our times together are usually concluded with ten to twenty minutes of corporate prayer that are often marked by a holy and powerful sense of God's presence.

Second, the Lord directed me to preach a series of messages entitled "PrayFirst" from Matthew 6:5-15. Week after week I spoke from this passage teaching our people how to pray using the Lord's Prayer as a model and guide for prayer times. Often people are told to pray but do not know how to pray. So, I tried to teach them simple but strong principles to help them pray effectively. You can find some of those messages on prayer in video form on my YouTube channel.[79]

79. YouTube.com/davidestewartjr.

Hungry for His Presence

Third, from the very beginning of my tenure as pastor of NewLife Church, I took time during our Sunday Morning Celebration Services to lead our church family in extended times of praise and prayer. We don't just have a perfunctory pastoral prayer time. We call out to God with zealous and faith-filled intercession. Sometimes I invite members from the congregation to come and help lead in the prayer times.

One visitor remarked, "When you first started praying and continued for some time, I thought that you may be going too long, but then I realized that you and the people were really praying—not just talking." She was sincerely impressed and blessed by our prayer time.

Several remarkable testimonies have come from our times of prayer. People have testified that they or loved ones have been healed. Others have been saved. During one such time of prayer, God miraculously healed a woman of barrenness. She and her husband recently brought the precious baby girl God gave them for baby dedication.

There have been many other things we have done to emphasize prayer, but there are two last important prayer exercises we have practiced that I want to mention. One, I have directed our associate pastors to open the services with three to five minutes of prayer as the people come into the sanctuary. We want the Holy Spirit's presence from the very beginning of the service.

Finally, we have asked our people on at least two occasions to write the names of unsaved people on a piece of paper that they then brought forward and laid on the platform. We prayed over those names, and have kept the papers at the front of the church continuing to pray for the people mentioned. More than one person has come to the church and been saved or recommitted their life to the Lord after such prayer.

Prayer is a key to experiencing the presence of God in your life and in your church. Do you want the presence of God? You must pray. When you have prayed, pray more. Then, continue praying. God will hear and answer His people's prayers.

Chapter 16

Where Is Joy Found?

Walk downtown on a Friday night. Stroll by the bar and grill, sports bar, or any other establishment known for its food and drink. Low lights, the flash of a smile, a throaty laugh, the odors of adult beverages and fried foods, a flirtatious look, and a thousand other symbols, signs, and signals indicate that you are in the fun zone, the good times area, and the laid back "'forget your troubles" part of town. Fun for an hour or two—but is joy really found there?

Just a few blocks away, rising high above the surrounding houses, looms a giant stadium. Bright lights and loud music advertise its existence and purpose. Roaring throngs and cheering fans swarm its hallways, stairwells, and cavernous seating areas a few weeks out of the year. Some come with children, their flags waving and their faces painted. They arrive like tribal worshipers entering a pagan ceremony. Others, scantily dressed, shout ugly obscenities, down quarts of beer, and drunkenly offer blaring commentaries on the game as if they were ancient warriors engaged in battle. Fun? Yes, at least it is sold for such. Each fan spends exorbitant amounts of hard earned money for a few hours at the ballgame. Entertaining—but is joy found there?

The list of places, parties, or programs that offer solace, relaxation, and fun are many—but is joy found in any of those places or things? Where is real, lasting joy found?

In this last chapter, let's look at Psalm 16 to discover where joy *is* found. God wants His children to walk in joy, but there is only one place where joy, lasting and real joy, can be found—in the presence of God.

> *Psalm 16*
> *Preserve me, O God, for I take refuge in You.*
> *I said to the Lord, "You are my Lord;*
> *I have no good besides You."*
> *As for the saints who are in the earth,*
> *They are the majestic ones in whom is all my delight.*
> *The sorrows of those who have bartered for another god will be multiplied;*
> *I shall not pour out their drink offerings of blood,*
> *Nor will I take their names upon my lips.*
> *The Lord is the portion of my inheritance and my cup;*
> *You support my lot.*
> *The lines have fallen to me in pleasant places;*
> *Indeed, my heritage is beautiful to me.*
> *I will bless the Lord who has counseled me;*
> *Indeed, my mind instructs me in the night.*

David Stewart

I have set the Lord continually before me;
Because He is at my right hand, I will not be shaken.
Therefore my heart is glad and my glory rejoices;
My flesh also will dwell securely.
For You will not abandon my soul to Sheol;
Nor will You allow Your Holy One to undergo decay.
You will make known to me the path of life;
In Your presence is fullness of joy;
In Your right hand there are pleasures forever.

Psalm 16 is a messianic psalm that speaks of our Lord. It depicts His deep devotion, His death, and His resurrection. Peter quoted this psalm when he preached on the day of Pentecost announcing that it was written by David in a prophetic description of Jesus.[80]

Psalm 16 is also a reflection on David's life. He speaks of his servitude, worship, and total surrender to God. David expresses his utter confidence and trust in the Lord; in doing so, he points us to the joy that we so long to know and experience.

So, where is joy found? Joy is found in a relationship with God. The psalmist says, *"I take refuge in You."*[81] David understood that a relationship with God is foundational to a life of joy. One cannot have joy without knowing God through faith in Jesus.

80. See Acts 2:25-28.
81. Psalms 16:1

Hungry for His Presence

Second, joy is found in belonging to God. David delights in saying that the Lord is his God. Do we delight in expressing our dedication to God? Do we rejoice in announcing to the world and to God that we are His? The world does not hesitate to announce which beer they drink, team they support, or celebrity they follow. Do you take such joy in your relationship with God?

Then, David steps back and paints a contrasting picture. He expresses the vast difference between those who know the eternal, everlasting God and those who run after the temporal and seek after idols made by men's hands. Verse four describes the suffering or the sorrow of those who do not know God. They offer drink offerings of blood to idols and run to other gods to seek pleasure in things that never satisfy. Their lives are marked by emptiness, degradation, and degenerate behavior.

The psalmist not only reflects on the vanity of the worship and actions of ungodly people, but he says that he will not participate in their evil ways or mention the names of those gods that the heathen esteem. Do we try to replicate the evil things of this world hoping to draw sinners into our churches? Does it bring glory and honor to God or create hunger for God in the hearts of those who are far from Him when we mention the names of rock stars, show movie clips, or make reference to evil or empty behavior in our messages? Those things are worthless, offensive to God, and cannot satisfy joyless hearts.

Joy is found in making Jesus the focus of your greatest desires—whole-heartedly pursing a relationship with Him. In verse five, David says, *"The Lord is the portion of my inheritance."* David found his value and worth in his relationship with God. Do you truly feel like your wealth and heritage are found in the Lord?

People associate luxury cars, big houses, or boats with wealth. They base their worth and find their identity in their possessions. They think that the accumulation of wealth will satisfy them and impress others.

Where do you find your satisfaction? Do you look to temporal things or pleasures, hoping that others will think you are successful because of your toys or tokens of worldly wealth?

Joy is found in communion with God. In verse five the psalmist also declares that the Lord is his cup. This cup symbolizes refreshing. To what or to whom do *you* look for refreshment when you are weary? Do you look to entertainment, sports, or vacation? Those things may rest your physical body, but they do not restore your soul. Worldly indulgences cannot satisfy the thirsting of your spirit. Jesus says to those who are thirsty, *"If anyone is thirsty, let him come to Me and drink."*[82]

In verse six, David paints a picture of utter and complete satisfaction and fulfillment. *"The lines have fallen to me in pleasant places; indeed, my heritage is*

---

82. John 7:37

beautiful to me." David was contented with life, his position in life, and all that had been given to him. Through this verse, we learn that we can have total satisfaction through our relationship with Christ.

Do you find your satisfaction in Jesus? Or, is He just the one you look to in an emergency, the one you call on when you are hurt, or the one you have a casual acquaintance with once a week at church? Is He just an ephemeral answer to problems, or is He your eternal satisfaction? Do you find your fulfillment in things or in Christ?

Joy is found in devotion to God. In verse eight, the psalmist says, *"I have set the Lord continually before me."* Look to the Lord at all times. Do you look to money for joy? Do you seek possessions or advancement in your job as signs of your success, or do you look to the Lord? Do you look to see the sign of approval in His loving eyes? Satisfaction is found in continually seeking the Lord.

This satisfaction and contentment leads to great assurance. Verse ten reads, *"You will not abandon my soul to Sheol; nor will you allow your holy one to undergo decay."* Difficult times may come. Problems may arise, but I know that He will not leave me in the pit or in the dungeon of despair. He will not forsake me; therefore, *"My heart is glad and my glory rejoices."*[83] Followers of Jesus have joy that cannot be shaken.

---

83. Psalms 16:9

David Stewart

I have followed the path of life that is found in Christ Jesus. My joy is discovered in the presence of God as a result of knowing Christ. Joy is a fruit of continually seeking His face and a reward of regularly dwelling in His presence.

Yes, I can agree with the psalmist that in God's *"right hand there are pleasures forever."*[84] That is where my joy is found. Joy comes from the gracious and loving hand of God.

This is what we must teach in our churches and inscribe in the hearts of believers. Joy is not found in the temporal things of earth. Joy is not found in debauchery, drunkenness, or immorality. Joy is found in knowing and following Jesus. Joy is found in seeking His face and living in His presence. Joy is found in Him! David concludes this psalm saying, *"You will make known to me the path of life; in Your presence is fullness of joy."*[85]

---

84. Psalms 16:11
85. Psalms 16:11

Conclusion

What Will Happen When He Comes?

What happens when His presence really fills our lives and our churches? As you have read through this book, I hope you have begun to feel a new hunger for God's presence. We need His presence. Do you long for His wonderful presence in your life, your family, and in your church? Are you hungry for the presence of God?

Yes, we desperately need a fresh touch and visitation of God's presence. The good news is that God longs to visit with us and dwell among us.

Yes, your nation and the people of your nation need churches that are filled with the presence of God. People can find entertainment, thrills, and hype elsewhere, but those empty things will never bring transformation to broken lives and families. Only the presence of God can change them, bring them real hope, and offer them eternal life. Amazingly, this can happen.

People will not come to our churches because of the skill of our musicians, the eloquence of our preachers, or because of the cool lighting. If they do come for those reasons, they will eventually leave as they came—broken, sick, and sinful. Churches thick with the healing presence of Jesus are needed in this day marked by teen suicide and an increasing number of opioid overdoses. People will flock to churches thick with the healing presence of Jesus.

People will flock to churches full of the presence of God. A church where the presence of God rules and reigns will experience the miraculous and people will encounter life-changing transformation.

So much happens when Jesus shows up. His presence brings healing. When He came on the scene, a man born blind was healed.[86] A church full of the presence of God will be a church where people are healed.

His presence brings deliverance. When He and His disciples pulled up to a shoreline bordering a cemetery, His presence brought deliverance to a man possessed with many devils.[87] People today need liberation from demonic bondage and life controlling substances and situations. Churches where Jesus is lifted up and where His presence is welcome will be places of deliverance and freedom.

His presence brings hope. When Jesus came to the house of a man whose daughter had died, hope was revived and the little girl resurrected.[88] There is so

86. John 9:1-12
87. Luke 8:26-39
88. Luke 8:40-48

much hopelessness in the world today; however, Jesus gives hope, purpose, and meaning. Preach Jesus! Honor Jesus! People will receive hope.

His presence brings cleansing. By encountering Jesus, a man covered with leprosy was cleansed.[89] The Bible uses leprosy as a vivid illustration of sin and helps us understand that sin makes people unclean before God. Sin, simply defined, is disobedience to God and His Word. People with addictions to pornography, other sexual sins, and any other area of disobedience to God are spiritually unclean. Thankfully, the blood of Jesus cleanses us from all sin.

He goes where He is needed.[90] He is not afraid or repulsed by people's need. Churches that invite Jesus' presence are often churches that make needy people feel welcome. Jesus comes in response to their needs.

He goes where He is invited.[91] Prayer from a humble and desperate heart catches His attention, and worship captures His heart. Have you invited Jesus into your services? He will come if you invite Him.

He goes where He is welcome.[92] Is He welcome in your church, in your family, and in your life? If He is welcome He will come in all His glory and power.

89. Luke 5:12-13
90. Luke 4:31-37
91. Mark 5:22-42
92. Luke 8:40

Hungry for His Presence

When churches begin to pray and sincerely seek for a visitation of His Spirit, our churches will experience renewal and our nation will see a revival. There is, however, one caveat—one word of caution. Spiritual restoration will come, but it may come at a great cost and sacrifice to some followers of Christ. Many will face real persecution. A few may die as martyrs.

Genuine revival will come when God's people earnestly desire it and seek God with sincere hearts. Renewal will not come cheaply or as a result of frivolous worshipers dancing at the altar of narcissism and hedonism. There is the cost of sacrificial and earnest prayer. Men and women, children and young people calling out to God as they sincerely lay themselves before Him will experience His presence.

Followers of Christ must decide that they want His presence more than wealth, social acceptance, or worldly influence. They will become so hungry for God that they will devote themselves to prayer and the reading of the Word. His presence will become so precious to some that nothing else will matter.

If we get hungry for His presence, He will send revival. Revival is going to come, and when such a renewal comes our churches will be filled with people who are filled with the Spirit of God. It is going to happen because God says that it will. He has said that He will pour out His Spirit in the last days on people of every race, nation, and language:

David Stewart

It will come about after this
That I will pour out My Spirit on all mankind;
And your sons and daughters will prophesy,
Your old men will dream dreams,
Your young men will see visions.
Even on the male and female servants
I will pour out My Spirit in those days.[93]

God has promised to pour out His Spirit, filling His people with His presence. When His people repent of their sins, humble themselves, hunger for Him, pray, and seek His face, then He will fill our hearts, touch our children and students, heal broken people, and reveal Himself in power and glory to us.

God revealed Himself to Moses and the people of Israel when they had repentant hearts and cried out for His presence. If God rewarded them, I believe He will reward us too.

In closing, please pray with me:

> God, please fill us with Your holy
> presence. Mercifully create a hunger
> in us for more of You. In Jesus' name
> we ask it and believe it will happen.
> Thank You, amen!

---

93. Joel 2:28-29

About the Author

Pastor David E. Stewart, Jr. and his wife, Lisa Ann Stewart, have three children—Andrea, Tiffany, and Elijah—a son-in-law Nathan, and a grandson David.

Lisa and David have served with their family in a wide variety of roles and ministries. Their ministry has taken them to many different nations and given them opportunity to interact closely with godly and influential spiritual leaders from around the world. Today, David is the lead pastor of NewLife Church in Leominster, Massachusetts.

David is a proven ministry leader who is a skilled communicator and a passionate preacher of the gospel. His preaching and his writing are expressions of his personal relationship with Jesus Christ through daily Bible study and prayer. David is called to be a disciple of Jesus Christ. He is passionate about leading others to become disciples through evangelism, training processes, and mentoring relationships. He describes his purpose in life as "introducing as many people as possible to the Lord Jesus with the goal of helping them to become His followers and His disciples."

David can be contacted at pastor@newlifema.com.

We are a Christian-based publishing company that was founded in 2009. Our primary focus has been to establish authors.

"5 Fold Media was the launching partner that I needed to bring *The Transformed Life* into reality. This team worked diligently and with integrity to help me bring my words and vision into manifestation through a book that I am proud of and continues to help people and churches around the world. None of this would have been possible without the partnership and education I received from 5 Fold Media."

- Pastor John Carter, Lead Pastor of Abundant Life Christian Center, Syracuse, NY, Author and Fox News Contributor

The Transformed Life is foreworded by Pastor A.R. Bernard, received endorsements from best-selling authors Phil Cooke, Rick Renner, and Tony Cooke, and has been featured on television shows such as TBN and local networks

5 Fold Media
5701 E. Circle Dr. #338, Cicero, NY 13039
manuscript@5foldmedia.com

Find us on Facebook, Twitter, and YouTube

Discover more at www.5FoldMedia.com.

CPSIA information can be obtained
at www.ICGtesting.com
Printed in the USA
FFOW04n2232240418
46351283-47992FF

9 781942 056560